ROUTLEDGE LIBRARY EDITIONS:
DEVELOPMENT

INTERNATIONAL FINANCE AND LATIN AMERICA

INTERNATIONAL FINANCE AND LATIN AMERICA

STEPHANY GRIFFITH-JONES

Volume 36

Routledge
Taylor & Francis Group
LONDON AND NEW YORK

First published in 1984

This edition first published in 2011
by Routledge

Simultaneously published in the USA and Canada
by Routledge

Published 2014 by Routledge
2 Park Square, Milton Park, Abingdon, Oxon OX14 4RN
605 Third Avenue, New York, NY 10017

Routledge is an imprint of the Taylor & Francis Group, an informa business

First issued in paperback 2013

British Library Cataloguing in Publication Data
A catalogue record for this book is available from the British Library

ISBN 13: 978-0-415-58414-2 (Set)
ISBN 13: 978-0-203-84035-1 (ebk)(Set)
ISBN 13: 978-0-415-59386-1 (hbk)(Volume 36)
ISBN 13: 978-0-203-83850-1 (ebk)(Volume 36)
ISBN 13: 978-0-415-84524-3 (Paperback)

Publisher's Note
The publisher has gone to great lengths to ensure the quality of this reprint but points out that some imperfections in the original copies may be apparent.

Disclaimer
The publisher has made every effort to trace copyright holders and welcomes correspondence from those they have been unable to contact.

International Finance and Latin America

STEPHANY GRIFFITH-JONES

CROOM HELM
London & Sydney

Croom Helm Ltd, Provident House, Burrell Row,
Beckenham, Kent BR3 1AT
Croom Helm Australia, First Floor, 139 King Street, Sydney,
NSW 2001, Australia

British Library Cataloguing in Publication Data

Griffith-Jones, Stephany
International finance and Latin America.
1. Finance – Latin America
I. Title
332'.098 HG185.L3

ISBN 0-7099-1185-8

CONTENTS

To Eduardo Rodrigo and to all children,
in the hope that this generation will leave them
a better world than the one they inherited

ABBREVIATIONS

AID	Agency for International Development
BIS	Bank for International Settlements
CEPAL	This is how it is best known, in fact in English it stands for Economic Commission for Latin America (ECLA)
CFF	Compensatory Financing Facility
COMECON	Council for Mutual Economic Aid (Socialist nations)
DAC	Development Assistance Committee
GDP	Gross Domestic Product
IDA	International Development Association
ILLR	International Lender of Last Resort
IMF	International Monetary Fund
LDC	Less Developed Country
LIBOR	London Inter-Bank Offer Rate
ODA	Official Development Assistance
OECD	Organisation for Economic Co-operation and Development
OPEC	Organisation of Petroleum Exporting Countries
SDR	Special Drawing Right
UNCTAD	United Nations Conference on Trade and Development
USAID	United States Agency for International Development

FOREWORD

Several years ago, the Latin American Association of Development Financing Institutions (ALIDE) established its yearly Latin American Contest on Development Banking aimed at furthering research works and analyses on topics relating to the problems of development financing in Latin America and the role that Latin American development banking should perform.

In the 1983 selection process, the Jury, made up of the members of ALIDE's Executive Board, declared as the winning research work of the IX Contest, the one submitted by Stephany Griffith-Jones, a Chilean economist, who is at the present time Research Fellow at the Institute of Development Studies of the University of Sussex, England. This study, originally entitled 'Changes in International Finance and its Effects on Latin America: Past Trends and Future Prospects', fitted precisely one of the proposed subjects, namely 'Current Situation and Future Prospects of External Financing for Latin American Development'.

The above-mentioned research, presented here, studies the problems of external financing for Latin America from a historical viewpoint and, particularly, analyses the external debt service difficulties that Latin American countries are facing and the impact that they have or may have on both developing and industrial countries.

The increased and justified concern about this problem becomes apparent since the difficulties of Latin American countries to service their external debt may cause a curtailment or restriction of financial flows towards them and, consequently, may bring about lower progress in terms of economic growth and living standards in the region. From the industrial countries' perspective, the concern is based on the negative impact that potential defaults or arrears and debt reschedulings may have on the industrial countries' private banks. In other words, these concerns are related to the most severe economic crisis currently being faced by Latin America, and the potential crisis of the industrial countries' banking system.

This study devotes a chapter to discussing the international financial flows within a broad theoretical framework. In this respect, it examines the debates that preceded the establishment of the Bretton-Woods system, emphasising the contribution of John Maynard Keynes. It also examines the main features of the international monetary system as well as its limitations and contradictions, particularly regarding their impact on developing economies.

The second part of this study is intended to analyse the evolution of international financial flows towards Latin America since the Second World War and their implications on national development targets. In this analysis, the author focuses not only on the quantitative trends but also describes the main forces which brought about these flows. It should be noted that a greater emphasis is given to the analysis of the features prevalent during the seventies and the early eighties.

The author asserts that the analysis of the evolution of international financial flows towards our region contributes to identify in each decade following the Second World War, a new actor that had an important role in providing new financial resources: foreign investors in the fifties, official aid agencies in the sixties, and international private banks in the seventies. As is stated in one of the study's hypotheses, one of the most problematic aspects in the eighties is the lack of such an actor willing and able to assume a dynamic role in generating external financing for developing countries.

The study then goes on to examine the recent evolution of Eurocredits markets, whose significant enlargement has taken place concurrently with a growing 'privatisation' of developing countries' debt structure, particularly in Latin America. Also, it looks at the crucial role that the International Monetary Fund should perform in Latin American countries' external debt reschedulings.

The last part of the study contains the main conclusions as well as some proposals for reforming the international financial and monetary system. It concludes that the future prospects for external financing of developing countries will not be very encouraging while the current economic and financial trends follow the pattern prevalent in the early eighties. In this connection, it is stated that if the world recession continues, private financing flows are expected to grow slowly or even decrease because of reluctance by these lending sources to expose additional financial resources, particularly in major debtor countries.

In searching for an adequate provision of external financing for developing countries, this study discusses a number of possible measures to be taken into account, being grouped as follows: (a) measures to maintain, particularly in the short and medium terms, private lending flows, and to attempt to create new mechanisms in order to make private financial flows more appropriate to the needs of developing countries; (b) measures to sustain or increase the role of multilateral official institutions; (c) increased South-South co-operation, possibly through the creation of new institutions; and (d) restructuring existing debt. It is asserted that some of the proposals discussed in items (b) and (c) and, possibly to a smaller extent, in (a), are linked to the search of a new dynamic actor willing and able to provide adequate financial flows towards the developing world, particularly to Latin America.

Finally, ALIDE wishes to express its satisfaction in the publication of this study as well as its acknowledgement to Croom Helm Publishers for their interest in making this valuable study available. In this way, our institution hopes to accomplish one of the main aims of the Contest, that is, to make the winning research works widely known, in this case within the English-speaking segment of the international financial community, with the purpose of encouraging the knowledge and discussion of important problems on development finance.

General Secretariat
ALIDE
February 1984

ACKNOWLEDGEMENTS

My interest and research on issues relating to external finance for Latin America began several years ago when I was working with Osvaldo Sunkel on the Transnationalisation project; I continued this research when working with the late Dudley Seers. I am very grateful to both Osvaldo Sunkel and to the late Dudley Seers for many valuable and stimulating discussions on this topic, as well as its links with broader development issues.

I have discussed issues related to international finance for developing countries with a number of colleagues and students, both at the Institute of Development Studies and elsewhere. I am particularly indebted for very useful insights resulting from discussions with Michael Lipton, Frances Stewart, Hans Singer, Reg Green, Susan Strange and Edward Brett.

I particularly wish to thank ALIDE, whose IX Latin American Competition encouraged me to pull together the different strands of my thinking and produce this monograph. I am grateful to Carlos Fortin for drawing my attention to the ALIDE Competition, and for his encouragement to participate in it, and thus to write this book. I also want to thank Danielle Hodges, who so efficiently typed this book.

Finally, I wish to express my gratitude to my family for helping provide the practical and moral support, which made it possible and enjoyable for me to be a 'working mother' at the relevant time.

Stephany Griffith-Jones
Brighton, Sussex

Money does not manage itself.

Walter Bagehot, 1873

The substitution of a credit mechanism in place of hoarding would have repeated in the international field the same miracle, already performed in the domestic field, of turning a stone into bread.

John Maynard Keynes, *Proposal for an International Clearing Union*, April 1943

PART ONE: THE GENERAL CONTEXT

1 INTRODUCTION

The debt problems of developing countries (and particularly those of Latin America) have since mid-1982 become the focus of worldwide concern. In fact, it would be fair to say that the problems of developing countries, and of Latin America in particular, never before aroused such an interest in industrial countries. A slightly cynical observer might conclude that the concern expressed in industrial countries, therefore, is not basically about the impact which debt and financial problems may have on the plight of developing countries, but is based mainly on the fear that debt problems in the Third World will have severe disruptive effects on the industrial countries' economies.

Latin American countries are especially large debtors, particularly to the private multinational banks. Latin American non oil exporting countries account for a very high proportion of total non oil exporting countries' debt, and have increased their borrowing more rapidly than others in recent years. As a consequence of these trends, the debt-service ratio (defined as payments of amortisation of all maturing debt including the short-term one, plus interest on gross debt, divided by the value of exports) is much higher than that of the rest of the developing countries and has grown faster in recent years. Recent estimates for the major Latin American borrowing countries (Argentina, Brazil, Chile, Colombia, Ecuador, Mexico, Peru and Venezuela) published in Morgan Guaranty's February 1983 *World Financial Markets*, project a debt-service ratio for 1983 of 117 per cent for those countries, compared with *only* 36 per cent for major Asian developing countries and *only* 58 per cent for major Middle East and African borrowers. If the roll-over of short-term debt is excluded, the debt-service estimates become somewhat smaller, reaching 56 per cent for major Latin American borrowers, 14 per cent for the Asian ones and 16 per cent for the Middle East and African ones. The latter figure was highest in Latin America for Argentina (88 per cent), followed by Brazil (67 per cent), Mexico (59 per cent), Ecuador (58 per cent) and Chile (54 per cent).

The recent wave of serious financial problems of developing countries leading to debt reschedulings, payment arrears and the danger that these may continue has caused concern in a variety of ways. First, there is the concern that developing countries' financial difficulties and inability to service their external debt may further restrict financial flows towards them, and that this will (or already has) lead to a curtailment of their economic growth and of the living standard of their population. This concern, which till fairly recently was applicable mainly to the poorest developing countries has now spread to some of the relatively more prosperous and formerly most dynamic economies in the Third World, particularly to those in Latin America. Thus, it has been estimated by CEPAL (*CEPAL News*, January 1983) that Latin America's Gross Domestic Product (GDP) fell in real terms in 1982 by 1 per cent, compared with an increase of 1.5 per cent in 1981 and very high growth rates in the 1970s. As a result, CEPAL estimates that Latin American *per capita* GDP fell by more than 3 per cent in 1982. Although several other factors (most of them linked to the recession in the industrial countries) explain this deterioration, the lack of sufficient international finance has since 1982 clearly had a very serious negative impact on Latin America's economic prospects. Linked to this perspective is the concern, more frequently expressed in academic circles, that the difficulties in obtaining external finance (and the increasing role which will be assumed by upper credit tranche – high conditionality – lending from the International Monetary Fund (IMF)) will not only constrain economic growth and development, but will also constrain national governments' autonomy in policy-making.

Secondly, there is the concern of the industrial countries with the negative impact which potential defaults (or continued reschedulings and arrears) may have on *their* private banks, and more widely on their economies. This concern, which had been expressed by some observers in the late seventies, has catapulted to prominence particularly in industrial countries, since mid-1982, when several large debtors started rescheduling their debt.

Though these concerns are naturally linked, they are clearly different. The former is basically concerned with the crisis in Latin American (as well as other developing countries') growth and development; the latter is basically concerned with the 'potential' crisis of the industrial countries' banking system. These different concerns lead to different types of proposals; the former, which concentrates on measures which will enhance the growth prospects of developing countries, is illustrated, for example, by proposals made by the Group of 24 at the International Monetary Fund's Interim Committee. The latter concern is expressed in proposals which increase the ability of banks to remain financially viable. This was clearly illustrated by the US government proposal, presented in Toronto at the 1982 World Bank/IMF annual meeting, to create an emergency fund which would provide private banks with a safety net in case of any major international financial crisis. Certain proposals attempt to reconcile both concerns and suggest measures which would deal with both the developing countries and the private banks' crisis; probably the most comprehensive amongst these proposals, presented in the Brandt Report-2, is appropriately entitled *The Common Crisis* (IBIDI, 1983). These and other proposals will be discussed further, and their potential impact on Latin American countries.

The next chapter (2) will deal with the discussion of international financial flows in a broader theoretical context. For this purpose, the debates will be examined which in the nineteen-forties preceded the establishment of the Bretton-Woods system and institutions, emphasising the contribution (both theoretical and practical) of John Maynard Keynes. There will then be a brief examination of the main features of the international monetary system as it emerged from Bretton-Woods as well as its limitations and contradictions, particularly regarding their impact on developing countries; reference will be made in particular to the so-called Triffin dilemma and its impact on international financial developments. Whilst discussing the more theoretical issues of international monetary questions, an attempt will be made to relate these to political relationships and developments. Even quite orthodox analysts hold the view that international monetary relations are more closely linked to political issues than other branches of economic theory. For example, A. Crockett (1977) points out the particularly intimate links between economic theory and politics in the field of international monetary relations.

Recently, in a very lucid article, H. Wallich (1983)[1] distinguishes three forces which have shaped the changes of the international monetary system since the Second World War: the role of theory in specifying the economic analysis underlying reforms and other developments; the role of experience related to the historic factors which influenced both theorists and men of action in their choice of action or creation on monetary reform; and market factors, or more broadly the state of the world, reflecting forces which impinged on the international monetary system often without being directly related to monetary affairs. It is noteworthy that Wallich concludes that the influence of theory was often outweighed by the other two elements.

At another level, the needs for external finance by developing countries will be examined, as perceived by different thinkers, highlighting the seminal contribution of Raul Prebisch (for example in 1959 and 1969).

Finally, Chapter 2 will briefly cover the extent to which the financial flows that *de facto* went to developing countries – and in particular to Latin America – were consistent with those countries' development needs.

Within the context of the previous theoretical discussion, including the description of the international monetary system and its limitations, the evolution of international financial flows to Latin America since the Second World War (Chapters 3 to 6 and 8) will be examined, and their implications for national development (Chapter 7). In the discussion of international financial flows, this book will concentrate not only on the quantitative trends, but will also describe the main forces which caused these flows; the analysis will stress particularly developments during the seventies (Chapter 5) and the early eighties (Chapter 8).

In the final chapter (Chapter 9), the main conclusions from the historical analysis will be extracted, with particular reference to the problems of the early eighties. From this perspective, different proposals for international monetary reform will be examined, with special emphasis on those affecting financial flows to developing countries. An attempt will be made here to understand both the logic and the feasibility of major existing proposals (such as those made by the UNCTAD Secretariat (1983), by the Brandt Commission (ICIDI, 1983) and more recently by the Commonwealth Secretariat (1983) in the context of the previous theoretical and historical discussion. In particular will be covered the need for new mechanisms, and possibly for new institutional agents, to complement or replace those which played with relative (though limited) success the role of channelling external finance to developing countries in the past, but are now increasingly unable or unwilling to do so.

The key hypotheses, whose validity is to be tested are the following:

1. The international and financial monetary system established at Bretton-Woods was an important attempt to promote multilateralism in a universal system, which would help to avoid many of the serious economic difficulties of the thirties. However it had numerous gaps and contradictions. In relation to developing countries, it did not create appropriate mechanisms and institutions to *channel a sufficient and sustained level of net external financial resources* to developing countries in deficit – from the industrialised countries or other developing countries with a large surplus – as these countries' growth and development would require.

2. This gap in the Bretton-Woods system and institutions was partly

filled by different participators in the economic scene, who perceived at a particular time that channelling financial flows to developing countries (and to Latin America in particular) served well their own economic and/or political interests. New participators seemed to appear in each of the decades after the Second World War (foreign investors in the fifties, official aid agencies in the sixties and multinational banks in the seventies), willing to play a dynamic role in generating new financial flows. One of the most problematic aspects in the eighties seems to be the lack of any such new participator willing and able to take on such a role, while those who did so in past decades seem unwilling to continue their involvement to the same extent. This may lead in particular years and for particular countries or areas to substantial net transfer of financial resources *from* developing countries to industrialised ones, with negative consequences for the growth prospects of those developing countries and for the world economy.

3. The unsatisfactory and insufficient nature of financial flows to developing countries (and in particular to Latin America), which have been brought into focus by the international recession and by widespread debt crises in the Third World, seem to make evident and urgent the need for major changes in the international financial and monetary system. These should both help sustain financial flows through existing mechanisms and institutions (though attempting to make their flows more appropriate to developing countries' needs), and explore the creation of new mechanisms (or even new institutions) which would provide the dynamism for the eighties. Such efforts for change at an international level must inevitably be accompanied by attempts amongst developing countries to increase financial co-operation amongst themselves, as well as – in the face of an uncertain and rapidly changing world economic environment – relying as much as possible on their own national resources.

Note

1. Henry Wallich has been a member of the Federal Reserve Board of Governors since 1974. Andrew Crockett is a senior official of the International Monetary Fund.

2 A THEORETICAL FRAMEWORK

One of the key issues facing the international economy, both at the level of theory and practice, is related to appropriate levels and mechanisms for international financial intermediation. The essence of the problem has been discussed by economic theory for a long time; however, the problem has become significantly more acute in the seventies as both current account deficits and surpluses, particularly of different categories of developing countries rocketed. Furthermore, the issues have become somewhat more complex as financial intermediation internationally has acquired new and more complicated facets, besides the still fundamental classical purpose of channelling savings into productive investment. As the superstructure of investments and currencies has become enormous and complex, as the world's needs have become more differentiated, the result has been that many more of the gross flows through the capital markets of the world today reflect financial decisions that are not directly tied to (nor do they necessarily lead to) physical capital formation, than occurred in the past.

Several analysts, for example, Roosa (1983) argue that at present there is lacking an all-embracing theoretical understanding of the economics of international capital flows and their links with trade movements, which can come as close to fitting the conditions of our time as the formulations of previous theorists (e.g. Alfred Marshall or John Maynard Keynes) fitted theirs. Given the lack of such a body of economic doctrine and the complexity of the forces affecting capital movements, an attempt will be made to outline here some of the main relevant theoretical elements available which it seems can help illuminate best both past and future developments in capital flows, with particular reference to flows to developing countries.

The problem of financial intermediation arises, at the national and at the international level, mainly because those economic agents which save are not the same ones which invest. Both nationally and internationally, if financial intermediation between net savers and net investors is not performed adequately, the effect will be to depress the level of output and income to the point at which the excess of savings is eliminated.

As Keynes pointed out,[1] at a national level, it will always be true that ex-post savings will equal ex-post investment. Similarly, at an international level, ex-post the sums of individual countries' balance of payments deficits and surpluses must always add to zero,[2] and *ex-post* balance of payments surpluses and deficits will have been financed (even though recently the mechanisms of finance have taken such unorthodox forms as voluntary and involuntary arrears on debt-servicing and payment on imports). The central issue in the international – following the parallel with the national economy – is *not* so much that the financing of surpluses and deficits has taken and will take place in an *ex-post* sense, but rather what *levels* of deficits are sustainable by the financing process, and what *level* of economic activity in the deficit countries and in the world economy can be sustained.

The level of economic activity is not only determined by the amount and distribution of financial intermediation, but also by the form of national adjustment to current account surpluses and deficits undertaken by individual countries. In particular, this book will focus on the much neglected issue of adjustment by surplus countries, as the level of those countries' economic activity will influence the necessary financial flows required to sustain a particular level of economic activity in countries with current account deficits.[3]

It is well known that Keynes attributed in a national context the existence of income levels, which implied high levels of unemployment of the labour force and spare capacity, mainly to lack of effective demand; he extended this analysis to the international context. Thus in 1942[4] he wrote the following – which seems again particularly relevant today given the current conditions:

> If indeed, a country lacks the productive capacity to maintain its standard of life, then a reduction in this standard is not avoidable. If its wage and price levels in terms of money are out of line with those elsewhere, a change in the rate of its foreign exchange is inevitable. But if, possessing the productive capacity it lacks markets because of restrictive policies throughout the world, then the remedy lies in expanding its opportunities for export by removal of the restrictive pressures. We are too ready today to assume the inevitability of unbalanced trade positions. It used to be supposed, without sufficient reason, that effective demand is always properly adjusted throughout the world; we now tend to assume, equally without suffcient reason, that it never can be. On the contrary, there is great force in the contention that, if active employment and ample purchasing power can be sustained in the main centers of world trade, the problem of surpluses and unwanted exports will largely disappear,

even though, under the most prosperous conditions, there may remain some disturbances of trade and unforeseen situations requiring special remedies.

After this analysis, Keynes follows on with his main policy proposal: 'There is no obvious means of offering a right measure of inducement to the general expansion of international trade except by a broadly based international organisation . . . the International Clearing Union.' Such a Clearing Union (whose main characteristics will be briefly described below) would have explicit and clear analogies with the development of the history of credit money at the national level, where the banking system eliminated hoarding by centralising savings and 'recycling' them to investors with positive results for all:

> Just as the development of national banking systems served to offset a deflationary pressure which would have prevented otherwise the development of modern industry, so by extending the same principle to the international field we may hope to offset the contractionist pressure which might otherwise overwhelm in social disorder and disappointment the good hopes of our modern world. The substitution of a credit mechanism for hoarding would have repeated in the international field, the same miracle already performed in the domestic field of turning stone into bread (Keynes, 1942).

The main characteristics of the international bank which Keynes proposed[5] were the following:

1. The bank (which he called Clearing Union) would organise a multilateral clearing of the bilateral imbalances between central banks, through which all international payments would be centralised and directed.

2. The operations of the Clearing Union would be carried out in a new international reserve asset (which he called 'bancor').

3. Member countries would be able to build up credit balances or draw on overdraft facilities with the Clearing Union. Interest would be charged both on overdraft facilities *and on excessive credit bancor holdings;* this latter proposal having the explicit aim to encourage *also* the adjustment of surplus countries, thus introducing a far greater symmetry to adjustment than then existed, and reducing as well the deflationary bias to the world economy which emphasis only on adjustment on deficit countries implied (and incidentally still implies).

4. Keynes's proposal implied a very large institution, which would allow unconditional access to large overdraft rights of at least US$26 billion, in which the potential US liability could have amounted to as much as US$23 billion.[6] To perceive the importance of this sum, in present terms, it seems interesting that, according to Williamson's recent calculations,[7] this would be equivalent in 1983 to a one-off allocation of over 720 billion SDR with no acceptance limit!

The US position in the debates previous to – and at – Bretton-Woods were significantly different to those of Keynes and the British delegation;[8] the US government's main aim was to create a fund that would 'maintain international equilibrium at a high level of international trade' and therefore to secure from members 'commercial policies designed to reduce trade barriers and to terminate discriminatory practises'.[9]

It is well known that in almost every case where the initial views of the US government differed from those of the British, the Fund's Articles ultimately reflected the former proposal, which was inevitable given the relative financial, economic and political muscle of the United States and Britain at the time. Thus, the post-war order established at Bretton-Woods implied:

1. A restriction placed on competitive exchange markets.

2. The gold-exchange standard would be perpetuated, without creation of any new international reserve asset (until 1970, when Special Drawing Rights were created).

3. There would be no effective adjustment pressures on surplus countries; the US delegation introduced a 'scarce currency clause', as a concession to the UK and other deficit countries, which allowed members to limit 'the freedom of exchange operations' in the currencies of a country with a large surplus. This amendment, which reflected partly a technical concern that the Fund might have otherwise been placed in the position of promising to provide a currency that it did not have, was also interpreted as a desire to meet British wishes for a guarantee of symmetry in adjustment pressures exercised by the Fund. However, in the event, the scarce currency clause was *never* applied, and so no effecive direct pressure has ever been applied by the International Monetary Fund on surplus countries.

4. Perhaps most important of all, the size of the Fund created was significantly smaller than that envisaged by Keynes. The size of the Fund

created was US$8.8 billion, with a US contribution of US$3.2 billion (as opposed to a minimum of US$26 billion and US$23 billion proposed in the Keynes Plan, see above). Although deliberately it was not made clear at the time, the US position was that lending by the International Monetary Fund, except on a very limited scale, should imply stringent conditions on the borrowing countries' policies. As has been clearly described in Dell (1981), conditionality was not explicitly introduced in the initial IMF Articles of Agreement ratified at Bretton-Woods, but was later introduced since 1952, as other countries conceded to US views.

Without doubt, the Bretton-Woods system (and the institutions it created, the IMF and the World Bank) implied a bold attempt at promoting multilateralism in a universal system with clear rules, which helped to avoid many of the serious economic difficulties of the inter-war years. As such, it contributed to post-war reconstruction and to the remarkable period of growth of world production and trade in the 1950s and 1960s; the international co-operation it achieved was significantly in advance of anything achieved in earlier periods.

However, the gaps and weaknesses of the Bretton-Woods system lead eventually to increasing contradictions, which implied the breakdown of the system in some of its specific aspects and to the curtailment of its contribution to the growth of world output and trade. It would seem that Keynes's theoretical and institutional vision would have implied a far more significant advance in the level of organisation of the international financial system, and would have helped to avoid many of the contradictions which emerged in the Bretton-Woods' system. It is noteworthy in this respect that major attempts at reforming or even replacing the Bretton-Woods system (i.e. the Triffin Plan, US government proposals for reform in the early seventies, the proposals in the Brandt Commission Reports) use elements which are similar (or are based on similar principles) to those contained in the original Keynes Plan; in particular, we are referring to the need for much more importance to be given to an international currency, larger public international financial institutions than those existing and some effective measures of exerting pressure on countries with current account surpluses.

Naturally, not all – or perhaps not even most – of Keynes's detailed proposals for an International Clearing Union would be relevant today in a significantly different world to that of the mid-1940s. Similarly, many of the contradictions which emerged in the Bretton-Woods system were not only because of the original limitations and gaps of this system, but because of its relative slowness to adapt to rapid economic and political changes. Amongst these changes are: (a) an increasing international interdependence (which makes individual national economies far more vulnerable to developments in other parts of the world economy, in areas such as large private capital movements across borders and increased synchronisation of business cycles amongst different countries), and (b) an increased number of countries and a significant growth in developing countries who are now major participators in global issues. This has led to a world economy with a multipolar character, which differs sharply from the post-war world where the US economy's importance was far greater than it is now.

In the preceding discussion Keynes's contribution to the debates on the post-war order in the field of international economic and financial relations has been highlighted. This has been done for two reasons: firstly, such a theoretical perception at an international level would have seemed to assure higher levels of world trade, output and employment and a more rational international economic organisation. Secondly, Keynes was concerned with protecting the interests of countries which – like his own, the UK, and most of Europe – would emerge from the Second World War with significant current account deficits and in need of restoring or reconstructing their economies. Many of those concerns ceased to be of much relevance to those countries after their economies recovered – and in several cases, even had current account surpluses for long periods; those concerns were, and still are, extremely relevant to the interests of developing countries, which by the very nature of their low incomes and their wish to achieve growth and development, tend to have almost in-built deficits in their balance of payments.

Most authors agree that the economic development process normally includes a requirement both for long-term external capital and for short-term balance of payments assistance to finance both long-term and short-term deficits of developing countries' current accounts; furthermore, most countries which are now industrialised (and particularly, the US, Canada, Australia and New Zealand) relied heavily on foreign capital and foreign lending for their development.[10]

It must however be recognised that there is little consensus among economic theorists and development practitioners about the *exact* relationship between external capital and development, even though most thinkers accept that external capital is necessary for accelerating development. In Latin America, amongst those most critical of the role of external capital because of its potential negative effects on national autonomy have been analysts, linked to the 'dependencia' school. For example, Sunkel (1969) wrote: 'it is in this aspect . . . the overbearing and implacable necessity to obtain external financing . . . which finally sums up the situation of dependency; this is the crucial mechanism of dependency'. It is noteworthy that even Sunkel – as well as many, though not all, radical thinkers – reluctantly recognise the need for external capital for development, even though they are critical of its effects.

On the other side of the spectrum, other theorists have not only asserted categorically the need for external capital in development, but have also attempted to quantify through a relatively simple mathematical model how much external capital should be transferred to a developing country and at what rate the capital could be absorbed. An influential study along these lines was that of Hollis Chenery and Alan Strout (1966), which was based on a 'two-gap' model (the gaps referred to are those resulting from comparing investment needs with projected domestic savings, and import needs with projected exports). Although this approach was useful for highlighting the role of external capital in development, it has later been criticised for its excessive and almost mechanical emphasis on foreign exchange as the sole constraint on development, and its concentration on the aggregate level – and neglect of sectoral considerations.

A more balanced approach to the link between external capital and development can be found, for example, in the writing of Raul Prebisch, whose thinking on these – as well as on other matters – has been very influential both worldwide and in Latin America in particular.

In his many writings and reports, Prebisch (for example, in 1959, 1964, 1979) pointed out that acceleration in the rate of growth of developing countries implies more than a proportionate increase in the demand for imports, as a tendency to external disequilibrium is inherent in the process of development. Prebisch emphasised, particularly in his earlier writings, that developing countries faced deteriorating 'terms of trade' because the demand for primary products had a lower growth rate than that for industrial products with the result that developing countries' export prices expanded less than that of the industrial goods which they required. In order to overcome this problem, developing countries embarked on a process of industrialisation which accelerated the demand for imports of manufactured and other goods, thus creating a serious bottleneck that, if not overcome, may inhibit development.

Together with other measures, taken both at a national and an international level, a transfer of foreign financial resources may play, according to Prebisch, an important role in helping to eliminate or control these financial disequilibria. Prebisch stresses in his writings (see, for example, Prebisch 1979:24) that several conditions must be met for such flows to contribute to development. These are: (a) the net volume of foreign flows must be appropriate to the development needs, (b) the outflows generated for payments of profits and interests must still allow for future net flows; it is therefore desirable that the financial terms of such flows (in relation to maturities, grace period and level of interest rate) are not too onerous, and (c) the net external financial flows are used for investments which will contribute to an increase in exports and/or a substitution of imports.

Prebisch also has stressed that the role of net foreign financial flows towards Third World countries will make a positive contribution towards their development, if they are accompanied by other measures, both nationally and internationally. At a national level, he emphasises measures that will improve income distribution, which will broaden markets for industrial development; internationally, he has stressed, for example, measures which will give access to exports of industrial products from developing countries, both in industrial countries and in other developing countries.

It can, therefore, be concluded that for Third World countries to grow and develop rapidly there is a widely recognised need for them to obtain a sustained net flow of external financial resources, on terms which are not excessively onerous; the sources from which such funds would originate are the industrialised countries or other developing countries with large surpluses (e.g. oil exporting countries that have experienced large oil price rises).

As mentioned above, the proposals which preceded the creation of the Bretton-Woods institutions (in particular Keynes's proposals) implied that the channelling of such flows to developing countries would have been, to an important extent, carried out through a central public international financial institution. The net contribution of the Bretton-Woods institutions to the financing of the large developing countries' current account deficits has been relatively limited, particularly so when those deficits increased dramatically during the seventies.

As the needs for financing current account deficits of developing countries were covered only to such a small extent by the Bretton-Woods institutions, and as different economic and/or political agents perceived channelling financial flows to Third World countries as serving well their own interests, such agents *de facto* played a major or dominant role in providing foreign exchange to developing countries in general, and to Latin America in particular. In the fifties it was the foreign investors pursuing greater profits which provided the main source of finance. During the sixties, official aid agencies – largely of a bilateral type – played the most dynamic role as in this decade aid was perceived to be in the interests of industrial countries, and particularly that of the US. During the seventies, the most dynamic participators were the multinational banks which rapidly expanded their lending to several Latin American countries in search of greater profits. One of the most problematic aspects in the world economy of the eighties seems to be the lack of a new participator, willing and able to play a dynamic role in the financing of the Third World in general, and of Latin America in particular. At the same time, those who played a dynamic role in former decades (e.g. multinational banks, official aid agencies) are very unwilling to continue to do so to the same extent as in the past.

In each decade after the Second World War, the flows were initiated mainly by institutions or enterprises based in the US, and then the process became 'internationalised' as institutions or enterprises from other countries increased their share in these flows; flows originating from US institutions tended, however, to play a major role throughout. The financing of these large capital exports from the US were, particularly in the seventies, not based mainly on a US current account surplus or a decline in US foreign exchange reserves, but were financed by a large increase in holding of US dollars by foreign official instittutions. US multinational companies, aid agencies and multinational banks were basically able to make such financial transfers because the rest of the world was (and is) willing to accept the dollar as an international means of payment and a store of value.

The type of mechanisms and institutions through which external finance flowed to developing countries generated problems for these countries which will be examined in the final section of this chapter; the reserve currencies in which these (and other) international financial flows were carried out also implied systemic problems, which will be discussed here.[11]

An international monetary system may be characterised by the arrangements made in five areas: management of the system, market availability, exchange rate regime, balance of payments adjustment and the supply of reserve assets. In this discussion here, particular reference will be made to the issue of the supply of reserve assets and its problems within the Bretton-Woods system; for reasons of space the other issues will not be examined in depth – though important, they are clearly of less relevance to our discussion. Such broader issues may be found, for example, in Crockett (1977) and Williamson (1977).

As discussed, a central feature of the Keynes Plan was its ambitious proposal for the creation of an international fiduciary reserve asset, bancor, in very large quantities and the virtually unlimited obligation of surplus countries to accept payments in bancor. The White Plan (which was the one adopted, given the realities of power) merely envisaged the creation of a pool of *national* currencies and gold from which deficit countries could borrow in limited quantities. In other aspects, the world supply of reserve assets remained unchanged – based on the gold exchange standard.

The gold exchange standard is a system under which reserves consist of gold and foreign exchange, which the reserve centre stands ready to convert into gold on request. When most countries are confident that the reserve currency will not be devalued in relation to gold, they hold a large proportion of their reserves in the form of the reserve currency rather than gold, as the former yields interest and is more convenient for transactions. A strong currency, widely used in international payments, is therefore likely to emerge as a reserve currency, unless the issuing country takes steps to discourage other countries holding its currencies in their reserves. While the reserve centre is concerned to maintain convertibility, the fact that its currency is serving as a reserve currency in theory should not avoid the need to maintain a satisfactory payments position, as failure to do so results in a loss of confidence which is liable to provoke requests for conversion of its currency into gold; in this sense, as Williamson (1977) pointed out 'the economic function of convertibility is, therefore, that of providing a discipline on the policies of the reserve centre, analogous to the discipline exerted by the threat of reserve depletion on other countries'.

After the Second World War, gold was the major reserve asset and was assumed to remain so; sterling was still the major reserve currency; the dollar was a reserve currency on a small scale in 1945, but its role expanded rapidly as the US overall balance of payments went into deficit and as the rest of the world perceived dollars as being as safe as gold and more convenient in terms of transactions and interest yield. The IMF did play a role in supplementing international liquidity, but a very minor one; furthermore, most of the limited liquidity available through the IMF was conditional.

During the 1950s, countries with a surplus converted part of their dollar earnings into gold and retained the remainder, the key problem then was defined as a 'dollar shortage'; in the early sixties the perception of the 'dollar problem' shifted from that of a dollar shortage to a dollar glut; the realisation began to emerge that as a result the dollar might not remain permanently 'as good as gold'. The essential contradiction of the reserve currency system was clearly articulated in Triffin's influential book, *Gold and the Dollar Crisis*. Triffin's central thesis was that the gold exchange standard contained an inherent dilemma that was ultimately bound to undermine the satisfactory functioning of an international monetary system based on the use of national currencies as international reserves. The 'Triffin dilemma' was clearly summarised by its author (Triffin, 1978):

> If the United States corrected its persistent balance of payments deficits, the growth of world reserves could not be fed adequately by gold production at $35 an ounce, but that if the United States continued to run deficits, its foreign liabilities would inevitably come to exceed by far its ability to convert dollars into gold upon demand and would bring about a 'gold and dollar crisis'.

There was of course a precedent in the problems of an earlier gold exchange standard (based then on sterling) which had collapsed in 1931, prolonging and intensifying the depression.

Academics, led by Triffin, began in the early sixties to search for a remedy to this dilemma, which many of them believed could be found by inventing a reserve asset whose supply could be expanded without the need for a US deficit. Probably the most daring of the major proposals was the one advanced by Triffin himself. A central element of the Triffin Plan was the creation of a new 'international reserve currency' to replace the traditional reliance on national currencies as international reserves; control over its supply was to rest with an international agency – a reconstituted IMF – instead of with national authorities. To phase out the use of national currencies as international reserves, existing foreign exchange deposits would be transferred to the reconstituted IMF in exchange for deposit credit there. The reconstituted IMF, however, was to be more than a clearing house for the settling of accounts. A second central element of the Triffin Plan was the suggestion of mechanisms by which the Fund could create new international reserves; these mechanisms were to be fairly similar to those by which national central banks create reserves for commercial banks. To allay any fear of excesses in deposit creation, special safeguards were provided for limits to their creation. The principles on which the Triffin

Plan was based were broadly similar to those suggested earlier by Keynes; however, the Keynes Plan had not specified the limits for the creation of new international reserve money, whereas the Triffin Plan had sketched clear ideas on how such limits should operate.

The academic discussions were later taken up at a more limited (or practical) level by officials in the Group of Ten (the meeting place of the industrial countries) and the IMF Executive Board. In 1967, there was an agreement to create a new reserve asset called the Special Drawing Right (SDR). Contrary to initial proposals from some industrial countries' governments to restrict the newly created reserves to an 'inner group of supposedly responsible countries' – the richer ones – it was agreed that such reserves should be distributed to all IMF members, in proportion to their share in Fund quotas, when an SDR allocation was made. SDRs relied for their acceptability on the fact that other countries were in turn obliged to accept them, which is the essential basis for the acceptability of money, rather than on support from national currencies or gold.

The agreement was a historic step, as it was the first time that a fiduciary reserve asset had been deliberately created by international agreement. Regarding the basic issue of stabilisation (that is the extent to which the international monetary system contributes to sustain high levels of economic activity at acceptable levels of inflation), the SDR did provide the international community with the ability to create reserves deliberately so as to avoid a reserve shortage, and made reserve creation independent from discoveries of gold or capricious variations in the payments imbalances of reserve centres. Its major limitation, which became crucially important during the seventies, was *in not providing a constraint on reserve growth through the deficits of reserve centres or the operation of the Euro-currency market*, because SDRs were created *in addition to, rather than a substitute* for gold and foreign exchange (here lies a major difference with the Triffin Plan). Another limitation, which has become apparent only in the early eighties, is that the decision to issue SDRs is *not* clearly linked to certain technical indicators, for example, level of world reserves, variations of world economic activity, but lies exclusively in the discretionary decisions of the governments, which constitute the required majority in the IMF's Executive Board.

The first SDRs were allocated to IMF members at the beginning of January 1970. The supplement to liquidity they provided was rapidly overshadowed by the outflow of dollars from the US initially reflecting the relaxation of US monetary policy and which fed on itself as confidence in the dollar waned. The massive increase in capital outflows from the dollar during 1971 implied that the value of holdings of gold and other monetary reserves in the US, which were sufficient at the beginning of 1971 to cover 32 cents in the dollar of its liabilities, declined to 18 cents in the dollar by the end of that year.

Triffin had been proved right in that the accumulation of US indebtedness to foreign central banks finally culminated in a gold and dollar crisis; the outcome did not lead – as he had feared – to a drastic reduction in international liquidity and a major recession. The US did not respond to the confidence crisis, as the UK had in 1931, by trying to maintain a gold exchange standard; by the time world confidence broke, the system had evolved into something much closer to a dollar standard, and the US was, therefore, able to suspend convertibility without curtailing international liquidity. What followed was, in fact, an explosive growth in dollar reserves that fuelled worldwide inflation rather than deflation, as the constraints – even though weak – which had been posed by the need to maintain dollar convertibility into gold were eliminated. Thus, the world reserve pool *doubled* from US$79 billion at the end of 1969 to US$159 billion at the end of 1972, 'increasing as much in this short span of three years as in all previous years and centuries since Adam and Eve; world reserves doubled again in the next five years' (Triffin, 1982).

The overwhelming source of this increase was foreign exchange holdings, of which traceable dollar and Eurodollar holdings accounted for more than 80 per cent, having risen nearly 20 times. The SDR and IMF lending contributed a small part of world reserves during the seventies; the marginal importance of SDRs in total foreign exchange reserves and in their growth is shown by the fact that *at the end of 1982 the SDR component was only 2 per cent of total reserves – including gold valued at market prices.*[12] This shows that the creation of the SDR though conceptually important, and offering a potentially significant advance for the international monetary system, has *de facto* made a marginal contribution to international liquidity.

In fact, it can be argued that as a consequence of generalised floating of the major currencies since the early seventies, and the resulting diversification of international reserves – both official and private – so as to reduce risk of currency loss, the international monetary system has *de facto* moved towards a multicurrency reserve system, that is at the opposite end of the spectrum from an SDR-based system, which the creation of the SDR had sought to establish.

The trend towards floating of currencies and a multicurrency reserve system, combined with the great expansion in international bank lending during the seventies, has given a new meaning to international liquidity, which to a certain extent became open-ended. Monetary authorities in industrial countries can enlarge their reserves by buying them in the market; even for countries – such as the developing ones – where this opportunity is not available, central bank reserves could – for certain countries and periods – be readily increased by borrowing from private banks; indeed, holding large reserves often made it easier for countries to borrow still more. Thus, particularly in the seventies, the supply of international liquidity became – for the industrial and middle income developing countries – in a gross sense virtually open-ended, subject to creditworthiness. As a result, international control of liquidity became largely a function of the market.

Therefore, it can be concluded that even after the creation of the SDR, IMF created liquidity, either through its own lending or through the issue of SDRs, has played a small role. Furthermore, the elimination of dollar convertibility by the US government in 1971 accelerated the trend of the main reserve currency centre – the US – to finance huge and persistent deficits mainly in its capital account by flooding of world reserves with its own IOUs. The main mechanism through which these reserves grew and were transmitted, particularly to developing countries, was through the expansion of international commercial lending to sovereign countries. Since 1982 debt problems and curtailment in net commercial bank lending – particularly to developing countries – are making evident the need for a major reconsideration of the role that private banks should and can play, both in the provision of global liquidity requirements and – to look at it from the other side of the coin – in the financing of countries' current account deficits, particularly in the developing world.

The specific problems created for developing countries by the nature of the mechanisms and institutions through which liquidity has been mainly created and transmitted to them in the last 30 years will now be discussed.

Different agents have *de facto* provided external finance to developing countries, and to Latin America in particular, when they perceived that this suited well their interests. However, when the channelling of new flows were perceived as no longer suiting these agents' interest (either due to changes in the developing countries or in the world economy), such new flows were naturally significantly reduced. As a result of such changes, net flows, or net lending to those countries (defined as disbursements minus principal repayments) decline significantly; net transfers (which measure net flows minus interest and profit remittances) *may become negative*, with harmful effects for these countries. In fact, this occurred in 1982 in Latin America, when total net capital inflows reached approximately US$19 billion and net repayments of profits and interests reached approximately US$34 billion,[13] leading to a negative *net transfer of US$15 billion for the continent as a whole during 1982.*

This dramatic change in net transfers is not only due to changed attitudes by lenders and investors, but is also influenced by changes in the international economy, such as an increase in interest rates combined with a relative reduction of developing countries' export prices. In fact, the relevant definition to measure *real* interest rates for developing countries is that of the nominal interest rates paid deflated *not*, as is conventionally done, by a price index which measures inflation in industrial countries, but by a price index which measures that country's export prices or even an index which reflects its terms of trade.

Furthermore, particularly in the case of international commercial credit, the flows have often been pro-cyclical, that is increasing when countries' balance of payments situation improved relatively, or when their prospects improved, and declining (or even becoming negative) when their balance of payments situation deteriorated; as a result the private banks have been called 'fair weather friends'.[14]

Because financial flows to Latin America did not correspond to a mechanism deliberately designed to suit the countries' and the world economy's needs, but were basically dependent on the changing perceived interests of the agents generating them, they tended not to be sustained at a level, consistent with the financing requirements of developing countries. In fact, during the sixties and seventies new flows – generated by the new dynamic participators – helped service the outflows corresponding to the actor that had played a dynamic role in the previous decade. This was particularly significant in the sixties, when new inflows of aid to Latin America (see Chapter 4) could be said basically to have coincided in magnitude with net outflows to foreign direct investors. Chapter 8 deals with the fact that in the eighties a rapidly growing proportion of new gross financial flows is directed to servicing previous loans contracted during the seventies. In fact, at the average type of terms (of maturity, interest rate and grace period) prevalent for Latin America and the Caribbean in 1981 for private lending,[15] gross lending would have to *double after six years* and *quadruple after ten years*, merely to sustain a constant level of net lending and to allow for servicing of the previous loans incurred.

Thus, gross financial flows have not been able to sustain adequate net levels for long periods as developing countries require; this has been linked to the fact that the financial terms on which most of them were committed (with the exception of an important part of aid flows) were inappropriate for the needs of developing countries, taking the forms most suited to the interests of lenders and investors. As a result, net transfers have often become either low or even negative. Therefore, it can be concluded that particularly in certain periods such flows did not fulfil the conditions set by Prebisch and other analysts fundamentally concerned with the Third World's development needs.

The search for new forms of financing developing countries' current account deficits and for generating more rational mechanisms of creating international liquidity should ideally take the following paths – sketched out briefly here:

1. New mechanisms should be created for credit flows, which do generate debt, *but* at much longer term maturities and at lower interest rates (hopefully fixed rather than variable) than existing commercial lending.

2. There should be renewed efforts for an expansion of *non-debt creating* mechanisms for increasing liquidity of developing countries. This could be best done in the short term by an issue of SDRs, and in the longer term by a greatly enhanced role for the SDR in the international currency system.

3. There should be some international control of less desirable and unstable forms of financing developing countries' deficits (and of increasing world liquidity), such as the expansion of variable interest and relatively short-term international private bank lending.

4. An increase would be desirable in the role of multilateral official development agencies, lending at relatively 'soft' financial terms, possibly combined with a far greater level of co-financing with the private sector.

5. A supranational forum (linked to the IMF) should be established which would review and determine overall and developing country liquidity needs as well as the mechanisms through which they are to be generated.

These proposals, their justification, as well as the technical and particular political difficulties for their implementation will be looked at again in the final chapter.

Notes

1. J.M. Keynes (1936).

2. In fact, there is a large 'errors and omissions' item in the World Balance of Payments Statistics, published by the IMF (see, for example, IMF 1983 *World economic Outlook*); this is due to imperfections and inconsistencies in the recording of flows and does *not* naturally affect the accounting equality, which always holds.

3. We are not discussing here the important issue of forms of adjustment by deficit countries, as it is not so central to our line of argument and it has been well discussed elsewhere – see for example, S. Dell and R. Lawrence (1980) for a 'structuralist' view and B. Balassa, (1981) for a 'neo-classical' view.

4. J.M. Keynes, 'Proposals for an International Currency (or Clearing) Union' (February 1942) in J.K. Horsefield (ed.) (1969).

5. 'Proposals for an International Clearing Union' (April 1943) in J.K. Horsefield (ed.) (1969).

6. Keynes had proposed an amount of 'say 75 per cent' of the average annual sum of each country's exports and imports during the three pre-war years. According to a contemporary estimate by Joan Robinson (1943), this would imply US$26 billion *as a minimum* – if not all countries joined.

7. Williamson (1983a) for this calculation considers both the growth of original member countries' GNP in nominal terms and adds the new membership of the Fund.

8. There are several good accounts of the debates in the literature; for different points of view, see F. Block (1977), Solomon (1983), E.A. Brett (1982); for the 'official' IMF view, see Horsefield (1969); the original documents presented at Bretton-Woods in Horsefield (ed.) (1969).

9. See foreword by H. Morgenthau (then US Secretary of the Treasury) to the White Plan of 10 July 1943 in Horsefield (ed.) (1969, 86).

10. A brief but interesting historical account can be found, for example, in M. Seiber (1982).

11. There is a vast literature available; one of the seminal books on the subject is Triffin (1960); another in-depth analysis of the issues is Williamson (1977).

12. Source: Commonwealth Secretariat (1983).

13. Source: *CEPAL News* (1983).

14. In this sense, it has been said that equity (direct investment) is preferable to foreign loans, particularly to finance investment in the export sector; when export earnings fall, so would the dividend repatriated abroad; for an early discussion of these issues, see Adler and Kuznets (1967). However, foreign direct investment has its own limitations.

15. Taken here are the average terms granted by private creditors to Latin American and Caribbean countries in 1981 (the last year for which data are currently available) based on World Bank data, published in *World Debt Tables First Supplement*, May 1983. These average terms implied an interest rate of 15.9 per cent, a maturity of 8.4 years and a grace period of 3.7 years. It could be argued that these terms were particuarly onerous due to the 'exceptionally' high interest rates during that year, and that the calculation exaggerates, therefore, the increase in gross amounts required. However, this is compensated for by the fact that it is assumed for the purpose of illustrative calculations here that in year one (in this case 1981) there was no previous accumulated debt, which obviously leads to an underestimation of gross flows required.

PART TWO: FINANCIAL FLOWS TO LATIN AMERICA

3 THE FIFTIES AND FOREIGN DIRECT INVESTMENT

As the Second World War came to an end, two developments had an important influence on the future nature of international financial flows: the creation of the Bretton-Woods institutions and the great weight of the US in the world economy.

As discussed in Chapter 2, the 1944 Conference of Bretton-Woods had agreed on the need for international consultation and co-operation on monetary matters. The two Bretton-Woods institutions – the IMF and the World Bank – were created as part of an attempt to avoid the instability of exchange rates, the financial chaos that had accompanied the world depression of the 1930s and the protective controls and competitive devaluations of the inter-war period. Bretton-Woods – and the institutions it created – represented the first coherent attempt at imposing order and stability on the world monetary system and preserving its unity as a single system. As Diaz Alejandro and Bacha (1981) have pointed out, the financial order emerging from Bretton-Woods, initially reflected the nineteen-thirties' disenchantment with *laissez-faire* in financial transactions which had then caused such negative effects; it was to a certain extent influenced by Fabian/New Deal notions.

It is important to note here that Latin American nations were the main group of developing countries to participate at the Bretton-Woods discussions and to join the Bretton-Woods institutions soon after they were established. Thus, 18 Latin American countries (Bolivia, Brazil, Chile, Colombia, Costa Rica, Cuba, Dominican Republic, Ecuador, El Salvador, Guatemala, Honduras, Mexico, Nicaragua, Panama, Paraguay, Peru, Uruguay and Venezuela) joined the IMF before the end of 1946, while only *eight* developing countries from the rest of the world joined at the time – they were China, Egypt, Ethiopia, India, Iran, Iraq, Philippines and Yugoslavia (IMF, 1982b). It is well known, that at the time of the setting up of the Bretton-Woods institutions, many of the countries today called developing were still colonies.

The attempt at the time to control the world monetary system by official international institutions was not accompanied in practice however by large financial flows from those institutions, particularly to the developing countries. As Lamfalussy (1981) has pointed out, the main feature of international capital movements during the years which followed the Second World War was the large outflow of funds from the United States. During the late forties and fifties, the United States was clearly richer and stronger than ever before, and was the only country able to offer both economic aid and military protection. Even though it controlled the Bretton-Woods institutions, the United States preferred bilateral channels for its financial flows. More importantly, the original Fabian Social Democratic notions which were evident at Bretton-Woods were increasingly pushed into the background once the war was over.

Since the Second World War, Latin American representatives had been appealing for a regional aid programme of substantial proportions, on similar lines to the Marshall Plan. Probably the most coherent and concrete of these Latin American proposals was elaborated at the 1954 Inter-American Economic and Social Meeting at Quintadinha, inspired by Prebisch and the thinking of CEPAL. The main proposals included the creation of an Inter-American bank, a level of annual foreign assistance and aid to Latin America of US$1 billion, the development of national planning and commodity price stabilisation. The proposals, as well as similar ones repeated later, were consistently rejected by representatives both of the Truman and Eisenhower administrations. The main reason (explicitly given in US official documents) was that Latin America played at the time a very secondary role in the Cold War. US officials recommended instead that Latin America concentrate on improving the climate for private foreign investment, basically through control of inflation, adhering *strictly* to what A. Schlesinger has called the 'theory of development as an act of immaculate private conception' (Schlesinger, 1975).

As a result both bilateral and multilateral official institutions played a negligible role during the fifties. As can be seen in Table 3.1 financial flows to Latin America were mainly in the form of private direct investment by multinational corporations. The import substitution policies of the Latin American countries provided them with profitable business. Investment was protected by high tariff barriers and credit was obtainable on favourable terms. Multinational corporations jumped the high tariff barriers in these countries by setting up or buying enterprises in the Latin American countries. This led to internationalisation of industrial production with important effects on the patterns of consumption in Latin America (Sunkel and Fuenzalida, 1979).

Table 3.1: US Capital Movements 1946-61 (US$ billion)

	1946-8[a]				1949-55[a]				1956-61[a]			
	Total	Europe & Canada	Latin America	Other Countries[b]	Total	Europe & Canada	Latin America	Other Countries[b]	Total	Europe & Canada	Latin America	Other Countries[b]
US capital (net)	–3.52	–2.54	–0.38	–0.60	–1.30	–0.60	–0.33	–0.38	–4.12	–1.65	–0.99	–1.47
Private	–0.77	–0.15	–0.32	–0.28	–1.04	–0.54	–0.24	–0.26	–3.30	–1.74	–0.69	–0.82
Government	–2.75	–2.38	–0.06	–0.32	–0.26	–0.05	–0.09	–0.12	–0.82	0.09	–0.30	–0.61

Notes: a. Annual averages. b. Including international institutions.
Source: US Department of Commerce, Balance of Payments Supplement (1961).

Table 3.1 shows that during the whole period 1946-61, US net private capital flows to Latin America were much higher than official ones; this was even more marked in the first ten years after the war, as during the second half of the fifties US official flows to Latin America began to increase.

In 1950 approximately half of US foreign direct investment was in the so-called developing countries, and over 40 per cent was concentrated in Latin America. The share going to developing countries systematically declined between 1950 and 1979 mainly as a result of the fall in the share of investment in Latin America (see Table 3.2). This decline was more rapid during the late fifties and sixties.

Table 3.2: US Direct Investment Position Abroad[a] (percentage composition, by areas)

	1950	1957	1966	1979[b]
All areas	100.0	100.0	100.0	100.0
Developed countries	48.0	55.1	68.1	71.6
Developing countries	48.0	40.5	26.8	24.8
Latin America	(40.6)	(31.4)	(18.9)	(19.1)
Others	4.0	3.4	5.1	4.6

Notes: a. Source: Data taken from ***Survey of Current Business***, US Department of Commerce (February 1981).b. Choice of years is based on those for which the information reflects a benchmark survey, whereas intermediate years are only based on sample information. For explanation, see O.G. Whichard 'Trends in the US Direct Investment Position Abroad, 1950-79' in ***Survey of Current Business.***

American flows to Europe show the opposite trend to those to Latin America. During 1946-8 it was official flows, through the Marshall Plan, which predominated. Large amounts of North American aid to help finance the reconstruction of post-war Europe was a mixture of US enlightenment and the pursuit of foreign policy interests; of special political importance was the American aim to stop the 'advance of Communism' in Western Europe. A similar political motivation led later to substantial increases of US aid to Latin America.

Private American investment in Europe grew very rapidly during the fifties and sixties, particularly as the incentive to replace and expand pre-war investment increased once economic reconstruction was under way. Furthermore, moves toward currency convertibility in Europe assured US investors that their income and capital could be largely or wholly repatriated.

The change in the distribution of North American investment

occurred in the context of rapid growth of total US direct investment abroad during the period 1950-79 (at an annual nominal rate of 10.1 per cent). Although American foreign investment was growing very rapidly, the share going to developing countries (and to Latin America in particular) declined substantially as US multinational corporations found more profitable and/or more 'secure' investment opportunities in other industrial countries, particularly in Europe. US direct investment in developing countries grew relatively more slowly during the sixties than in other decades. This was because of developments both in the industrialised and in the Third World countries. In developing countries the issue of foreign control became increasingly sensitive; this was reflected in expropriations and prohibitions of entry into sectors such as natural resources, telecommunications, etc. On the other hand, the US government imposed both voluntary and mandatory controls on outflows of capital to protect the balance of payments. Such controls particularly affected inter-company outflows.

An important trend which emerged in the composition of US investment during the period 1950-79 was that reinvestment of earnings grew while equity and inter-company flows declined; in fact during five of the 1972-9 eight-year period, absolute declines in inter-company flows were registered.[1] It is, of course, only the inter-company outflows which imply a transfer of financial resources to other countries.

The relative decline in the proportion of total US investment which went to Latin America, the diminishing importance of inter-company flows, as well as the rising level of profit remittances by US companies implies that already in the sixties the total net flow of direct private capital from the US into Latin America was a negative one. Thus, between 1961 and 1968, net direct investment minus profit remittances of US companies in Latin America amounted to -US$5.7 billion (Levinson and Onis, 1970: 120).

In the late forties and in the fifties private flows predominantly took the form of direct investment. The international financial and money markets had not yet recovered from the shocks they had suffered during the Great Depression. Private credit flows were small and mainly the result of credit provided by suppliers for the purchase of equipment. Thus, in Latin America in 1960, from the total debt to private creditors, 48 per cent was owed to suppliers (Inter-American Development Bank, 1979: Table 59).

This flow of private credit was induced by companies exporting capital goods or carrying out related equity investment in developing countries. Because of this close relationship with the corporations, it has recently been suggested that suppliers' credits should be considered as a variation of direct foreign investment (Billerback and Yasugi, 1977). But even if one disagrees with this categorisation, the fact remains that capital flows to Latin America until the sixties were mainly private investments by American corporations.

Note

1. See Table 3.2.

4 THE SIXTIES AND OFFICIAL AID

Towards the mid-fifties, the American attitude towards official aid began to change rapidly. As Christopher Prout (1976: 361) points out, '(the increase in aid) *motivation was unashamedly political*'. Americans believed that 'contributing to the economic and social development of the uncommitted nations would lead to the growth of societies sympathetic to their way of life'. The turning point for US aid to Latin America was the Cuban revolution in 1959 and the subsequent launching of a massive aid programme under the Alliance for Progress. Since the mid-fifties, a debate had been carried out within the US amongst 'internationalists' and 'isolationists' about expanded economic assistance, and this acquired importance during the 1957 hearings of the US Senate on the subject. On this occasion, the Committee on Economic Development, (a research-lobby group mainly made up of major multinational corporation executives and representatives of the press, created in the early fifties) strongly supported increased foreign aid. Again, in 1958, a major pro-aid meeting was organised under the telling title of 'Conference on Foreign Aspects of US National Security'; the transnationals were again well represented.

The violence that Vice-President Nixon met on his Latin American tour seems to have contributed somewhat to sparking off a response from Washington. In 1958, the American Administration accepted some of the Latin American proposals, the main one being to establish and fund an inter-American development bank.

There is agreement amongst different writers that the 1959 Cuban Revolution marked a qualitatively significant turning point in US attitudes towards Latin America, and this had a predominant influence on the magnitude and nature of aid, characterising the Alliance for Progress. Washington became increasingly anxious that because of Cuba's example and international efforts, revolution might rapidly spread through Latin America. It became fashionable to view the whole of Latin America as facing only two alternatives: reform or revolution.[1] The US needed to rapidly demonstrate a show of strength to ensure that the first prevailed. John Kennedy many times repeated that 'the promotion of democracy and reform were the ultimate answer to Castro and the Communists'. The new Administration believed that economic development and social reform, spurred by North American aid, could blunt the appeal of radicalism.

More broadly, the Alliance for Progress programme, and in particular, its initial rhetoric, was strongly influenced by a very important segment of Latin American thinking. The first blueprint for the Alliance was provided by the Quintadinha proposals. Particularly influential during the early stages of the Alliance, was the memorandum written by Prebisch, Mayobre, Felipe Herrera and other eminent Latin American economists and delivered to President Kennedy just before he launched his new programme. It called on the US to co-operate with those Latin American countries willing to make structural social and economic changes (with particular emphasis on land tenure, education and tax reform); to capture the support of the masses, by convincing them 'with clear and palpable evidence that the program is not motivated by a desire to create lucrative fields of investment for foreign private capital' and to launch an external programme of long-term supplementary capital assistance and commodity price stabilisation.

Thus, the initial rhetoric of the Alliance was very enlightened. As can be seen from President Kennedy's initial speech and from the Charter of Punta del Este itself, there were three officially stated goals to the programme: economic growth, structural change and political democratisation. Furthermore, it was said that structural change and political democratisation would be a condition for US economic aid.

Even though these progressive aims were the officially stated goals of the Alliance, the real aims pursued were somewhat different. As stated above, the Alliance (and the large increase in American aid which it implied) were to a great extent a reaction to the Cuban revolution; this is made very clear in the writings both of 'liberal' historians and politicians. For example, Levinson and Onis (1970) recognise that 'the predominant objective of US policy in the Alliance for Progress was to prevent other Latin American countries from following the example of Cuba'. 'Liberal' historians stress initial (though unusual and temporary) absence of corporate influence in the Alliance for Progress programme. They correctly point out that the programme, drafted by international civil servants, academic specialists and politicians, had hardly any reference to US private investment.

This attitude was not an oversight, but largely a response from the Kennedy Administration to the warning given by Latin American economists not to appear to be furthering investments of US foreign investors by means of the Alliance.

It should be pointed out, however, that big business was not as absent at the birth of the Alliance as the 'liberals' claim. Dillon who headed the US mission to Punta del Este was an international banker. One of the strongest defenders of the Alliance in the US Congress was the international banker David Rockefeller who, during that whole decade, headed the lobby of US business interests in Latin America. There had been a significant shift since the late fifties; North American big business, and in particular the multinationals, were clearly moving towards favouring and supporting an increase in US foreign aid.

After Kennedy's death, US policy towards Latin America became both more conservative and more fragmented. Thomas Mann, named by Johnson as both co-ordinator of the Alliance and Assistant Secretary for Inter-American Affairs, set forth the new line early in 1964. As Levinson and Onis say:

> What became known as the Mann doctrine consisted of four main objectives: (1) to foster economic growth and be neutral on social reform; (2) to protect US private investments in the hemisphere; (3) to show no preference, by means of aid or otherwise, for representative democratic institutions; and (4) to oppose Communism.

Thus, both structural reforms and democracy stopped being official aims of the Alliance.

By the end of 1966, US policy in Latin America was clearly in its more pragmatic phase, favourable both to the military and 'modernising' governments and democratic and 'reformist' governments. As the decade of the sixties drew to a close, the emphasis was shifting increasingly towards the 'modernisers'.

US business – and specially certain sectors – did not feel completely at ease with the Kennedy Administration and its Alliance programme. The change in 1964 was expressed by a top executive of the Standard Oil Company of New Jersey, who said 'Not until Thomas Mann came back in 1964 did the business community feel that it was "in" again with the US government.'

As shown in Table 4.1, the total level of gross US economic assistance to Latin America during the sixties was impressive, surpassing US$10 billion for the period 1961-9. However, net disbursements were substantially smaller. Over half of gross economic assistance was devoted to repayments, amortisation of previous loans and interests. American official credits and aid were supposed to finance government investment programmes. However, if the total financial flows between the US and Latin America are considered, it becomes evident that the *net outflow* of US private investment funds from Latin America to the

Table 4.1: Economic Assistance and Private Capital Flows between US and Latin America in the 1960s (US$ million)

Total gross economic assistance to Latin America 1961-9[a]	Total net US direct disbursements to Latin America 1961-9[b]	Total net flow of private capital from US into Latin America 1961-8[c]
10,286	4,819	-5,738

Notes: a. Includes all AID funds, Food for Freedom, long-term Export-Import Bank loan and other US economic programmes. (Excludes assistance from international agencies where US is an important contribtor.) Refers to obligations and loan authorisations. b. Includes same items as (a), but refers to net disbursements, less repayments and interests. c. Net direct investment minus profit remittances to US.
Source: S. Griffith-Jones (1979).

US (which includes net direct investment minus profit remittances) *exceeded the net inflow of US official funds*. This trend is perhaps the main factor explaining the support of US multinationals for the Alliance for Progress, even though it cannot be taken for granted that official aid financed outflow of foreign private capital.

Similarly to the initiative for foreign direct investment, that for the flow of official assistance came also from the US. As can be seen in Table 4.2, during the first half of the sixties, nearly all bilateral official flows to Latin America came from the US. US bilateral aid was then the largest source of net external finance for Latin America. Gradually, other industrial countries entered the scene, partly because the Americans wished to persuade their affluent allies to share more equitably the financial burden of allegedly common foreign policy objectives. American attempts to persuade its allies were mainly carried out through the Organisation for Economic Co-operation and Development (OECD); the establishment of the Development Assistance Committee there in 1961 was tangible evidence of such American pressure. When American interest in their official bilateral aid declined in the mid-sixties, other industrial countries (particularly the smaller ones) were increasing their aid programmes. As is shown in Table 4.2, by the mid-seventies US net official flows to Latin America were smaller than those from other industrialised countries – this contrasts sharply with the relative shares in the early sixties.

Similarly, multilateral development official flows to Latin America began largely at the initiative of the US government. It had a leading role in the creation and establishment of initial finance for both the World Bank in 1945 and the Inter-American Development Bank in

Table 4.2: Structure and Level of Net Inflow of External Resources to Latin America[a] 1961-8

% Structure	1961-5	Annual Averages 1966-70	1971-5	1976	1977	1978
1. Net public inflow	60.2	40.1	25.2	19.6	12.0	7.3
A. Multilateral	19.5	15.7	13.4	14.4	7.4	3.1
i. Development	16.6	17.1	11.6	6.6	8.4	7.2
ii. Compensatory	2.9	- 1.4	1.8	7.8	- 1.0	- 4.1
B. Bilateral	40.7	24.4	11.8	5.2	4.6	4.2
i. US	36.9	23.6	6.8	2.6	1.7	0.8
ii. Other countries[b]	3.8	0.8	5.0	2.6	2.9	3.4
2. Net private inflow[c]	39.8	59.9	74.8	80.4	88.0	92.7
A. Banks[d]	2.1	9.3	43.8	61.0	48.3	56.6
B. Suppliers	7.7	13.8	2.3	3.7	5.8	9.8
C. Bonds	5.0	2.5	2.5	3.3	14.8	10.3
D. Direct investment	25.2	33.3	26.2	12.4	20.1	16.0
3. Total %	100.0	100.0	100.0	100.0	100.0	100.0
Total actual level (US$m)	1,575.8	2,641.3	7,561.9	15,301.5	15,637.0	21,807.2

Notes: a. Includes the member countries of the Inter-American Development Bank and the sub-regional agencies. b. Includes the socialist countries and the OECD members except the US. c. Includes credits for nationalisation. d. Includes financial institutions other than banks.
Source: Calculations based on data in Inter-American Development Bank *Economic and Social Progress in Latin America 1979 Report*, Washington DC.

1959. They, too, acquired a dynamic of their own. Thus, although during the seventies the contribution of net multilateral development official flows declined relatively as a source of finance, their decline was much less than that of US net bilateral public flows.

To summarise, official aid in the sixties was predominantly an American initiative; it responded fundamentally to foreign policy interests of the US, even though the financial needs of Latin American countries played a part in the determination of the magnitude and composition of aid. Aid, albeit unintentionally, compensated for the net outflow of foreign direct investment. Finally, the US initiative was later followed – and surpassed – by other industrial countries. In the same way as foreign direct investment, aid became a 'transnational' initiative.

Note

1. See, for example, Schlesinger, 1975.

5 THE SEVENTIES AND MULTINATIONAL BANKS

Main Trends in External Financial Flows to Latin America

During the seventies four clear trends emerged in external financial flows to Latin America.

1. As shown in Table 4.2, since the late sixties the proportion of external finance coming from private sources has increased dramatically from 39.8 per cent in 1961-5 to 92.7 per cent in 1978. This implies growth of private net flows from an annual average of US$627 million in the period 1961-5 to US$20,205 million in 1978.[1] The relative and absolute increase of private flows to Asia and Africa also shows great increase, but not as spectacular as that for Latin America.

2. The second change is related to the composition of such private flows. As can be seen in Table 4.2, during the 1960s private funds were predominantly direct investments (though, as previously discussed, the net flow of foreign investment was already negative due to the outflow of profits). Since the seventies, multinational banks have provided the main source of flows and they have surpassed both direct investment and public funds. Net private credits from multinational banks have gone up from an annual average of US$246 million in 1966-70 to US$12,348 million in 1978, that is, an increase of *more than 50 times in a period of approximately ten years*. This feature follows the general trend for all developing countries but it is much more marked in Latin America, where a very high proportion of total credits have been concentrated. According to Bank for International Settlements (1981) data, in December 1980, of accumulated net total lending by multinational banks to non-OPEC developing countries, over 80 per cent went to Latin America. This rapidly growing proportion of net external finance arising from international banks has naturally led to the 'privatisation' of the debt structure of developing countries.

3. A third important trend is that, as shown in Table 4.2, during the seventies – and particularly since 1973 – there was a sharp increase in the nominal and real level of total net financial flows to Latin America. Although partly boosting foreign exchange reserves, these loans were mainly used to cover the growing deficits in balance of payments current accounts. As a result of the rise in the price of oil and of other imported goods, coupled with reduced demand for their exports due to

the recession in the industrialised countries, the current account deficits of Latin American countries (and particularly the oil importing ones) increased substantially. Thus, the current account balance of Latin America grew almost fourfold in two years, from US$3.5 billion in 1973 to US$14 billion in 1975; it increased dramatically again after 1978.

Table 5.1: Current Account Balance of Latin America 1972-8 (US$ million)

1972	1973	1974	1975	1976	1977	1978
-4,375	-3,492	-7,206	-14,058	-11,075	-11,209	-16,372

Source: as Table 4.2

4. A fourth new feature of financial flows after 1973 was that members of OPEC in some years replaced the industrial countries as net suppliers of capital, as can be seen in Table 5.2. Thus the shortfall of national savings over domestic investment in the oil importing world was met by the savings surplus of the oil exporters. The main conduit for 'recycling' this large volume of funds from surplus to deficit countries was the private multinational banking system of the industrial countries.

Table 5.2: The Pattern of Global Capital Flows[a] ($ billion)

	1967-73[b]	1974-7[b]	1978	1979	1980
Group of ten countries and Switzerland	-8¼	-¾	-19½	23½	51½
Smaller developed countries	1½	17¾	10½	12	22
Non oil developing countries	6	21	22½	36	51
Oil exporting countries	-1¼	-38	-4½	-68	-116

Notes: a. Total capital flows including monetary movements (i.e. current account positions with the sign reversed); minus signs indicate capital export. b. Annual averages.
Source: A. Lamfalussy (1981), based on IMF and OECD data.

The growth of Euro-currency markets and of their loans to developing countries

What were the main reasons that encouraged private banking credits to grow so rapidly that they became the most important single element in international capital movements in the seventies? An attempt will be made to describe the different factors that contributed to this change. As explained below, recycling of petrodollars since 1974 only accelerated a pre-existent trend. The entry of developing countries into the Euro-currency market will be examined, as well as the trends followed by this form of finance during the seventies. The criteria of 'credit-worthiness' will also be examined.

Growth of Euromarkets

Since the 1960s, most of the world's major banks have emulated other large corporations by becoming multinational. They established branches and subsidiaries outside their national borders at an unprecedented rate. In 1960, eight US banks had foreign branches; by 1975, 125 US banks had foreign branches. Total assets of US overseas branches jumped from $3.5 billion in 1960 to $181 billion by June 1976. Other large countries' multinational banking growth started later, but at a very rapid rate. Multinational banks' overseas operations are very concentrated. Thirteen US banks controlled in 1976 over two-thirds of all US bank foreign activity; the international earnings of these banks represented over 95 per cent of the increase in their total earnings between 1970 and 1975 (US Congress, Senate Committee on Foreign Relations, 1977: 9-12).

It was natural that banks all over the world should have become multinational to meet the needs of their multinational corporate custo-customers, who were increasingly investing and re-investing their assets abroad. The general expansion of world trade after the Second World War was an additional factor in the demand for growth of multinational banking. The role of the dollar as an international currency provided the base on which transnational banking developed.

Most analysts agree that this rapid growth of multinational banking is to a great extent attributable to the asymmetry between the stringent and detailed official regulations governing residents operating their own national currencies, and the great freedom of non-residents to operate in foreign currencies from the same constrained national banking system. (This would explain the fact that the transnationalisation of finance has outstripped that of production and that since the early sixties, the proportion of profits earned in foreign operations of total profits of US transnational banks has risen much faster than this same proportion for US transnational productive corporations.) Thus, the main centres of transnational banking have developed in countries where the least regulatory restriction was placed on their activity, and where more favourable tax treatment was granted.

In the late fifties, two developments had allowed multinational banks to move into Europe. In 1958, Western Europe returned to full current-account convertibility, particularly for non-residents. Authorised banks were allowed to take long and short positions in any currency. Increasing Soviet trade with the West generated dollars which the Soviet government preferred to deposit in Europe, to avoid a possible freeze by the US government.

A far stronger inducement to transnational banking growth was given by several US government regulations, introduced in the sixties to stem US foreign investment, in an attempt to improve the balance of payments. In 1964, the persistent US balance of payments deficit was in danger of increasing even more as a result of the over-heating of the American economy because of tax cuts accompanied by increased military expenditure abroad on the Vietnam war.

The Interest Equalisation Tax was introduced on foreign stocks or debt obligations acquired by US individuals and corporations. It stimulated US multinational corporations to deposit their earnings abroad instead of at home, and to finance new offshore investments through borrowing abroad by overseas affiliates; this trend was reinforced in 1968 by mandatory controls on capital exports of US multinationals. The 1965 Voluntary Foreign Credit Restraint Program curtailed short-term lending to non-residents located in the US, exempting from these ceilings their foreign branches and subsidiaries. US banks responded by shifting transactions from the home office to branches and subsidiaries abroad. Several Federal Reserve regulations encouraged US banks to hold foreign deposits offshore rather than in the US. Regulations put interest ceilings on time and saving deposits in US banks, again exempting offshore branches.

Even though many of these controls were terminated or diminished by 1974, undoubtedly they did much to expand offshore US banking. As one observer summarised: 'The American attempt to stop the export of capital in the nineteen-sixties led to the export of the American banking system instead.'

The main centre of transnational banking activity has been – and to a lesser extent still is – London. The main reason has been that when transnational banking developed, London was one of the world's main financial centres. Its large size was linked basically to the absence of regulation over a long period; banks in the United Kingdom could accept deposits and make loans in any currency but sterling (since 1979 also in sterling) completely free of regulatory restraint, because no interest ceilings or reserve requirements were imposed. In addition, private banks had confidence in the Bank of England as a successful monetary authority with one-and-a-half centuries of experience.

Other major centres provide a rapidly growing number of 'offshore havens', offering not only the absence of practically any form of banking regulation or oversight, but also strict banking secrecy and no taxation of foreign banks. Most banking transactions are still decided in the head offices of financial centres in the developed world. However, many are registered in the account of the bank's offshore branch (often in offices, with little more than a 'nameplate on the door and a receptionist to answer the phone'). These operations use a mechanism called the inter-bank market, which makes it easy for banks with a multinational base to minimise tax payments. The banks' 'booking procedures' may be compared to transfer pricing for other multinational corporations. In both cases, profit-taking is shifted from one sovereign tax jurisdiction to another, minimising the corporation's worldwide burden; this operation is simpler for the banks. Under changing conditions, finance capital flows more easily from one country to another than physical capital. Multinational banks have little physical investment and relatively few skilled non-mobile personnel; they can shift their operations and subsidiaries from one country to another in order to minimise tax payments, with greater ease and speed and smaller costs than productive multinational corporations.

The multinational banking market specialising in borrowing and lending of currencies outside the country of issue is commonly known as the Eurodollar market. However, the term Eurodollar is not very accurate. This market is no longer limited to Europe – the Far East and the Caribbean have a substantial share of operations. Neither does it deal only in dollars, even though this is still the major currency. In fact, a term such as 'transnational currency market' would be more precise.

The main final borrowers on this market are national monetary authorities, state enterprises, multinational corporations and official international organisations; however, most Euro-currency transactions are between banks. The majority of transactions are above one million US dollars. This international capital market offers two different types of finance: large-scale credits and bonds. The main difference is that the

Table 5.3: Size of the Euro-currency Market, 1964-1982

End of the year[a]	Net size of narrowly defined Euro-currency market[b] US$ billion
1964	12
1965	13
1966	16
1967	21
1968	20
1969	44
1970	57
1971	71
1972	92
1973	132
1974	177
1975	205
1976	247
1977	300
1978	375
1979	475
1980	575
1981	661
1982	686

Notes: a. Refers to December from 1964-1981, and to September for 1982.
b. Source: Bank for International Settlements (BIS), several *Annual Reports* and *International Banking Developments* (third quarter 1982). A problem of this series is its 'parochial' European nature. Its advantage is the availability of consistent statistics since 1964; there is no alternative consistent series available, which goes back to the sixties.
Broader measures of foreign claims of banks (such as the International Monetary Fund's IFS series) include, in addition to banks in industrial countries and offshore countries, the foreign claims of deposit money banks in many developing countries. In recent years, this measure has grown even faster than the figures in this Table. For a good discussion of Euromarket figures, see IMF (1982c).

latter have fixed interest rates, and are on the whole reserved for 'first-class borrowers'. Developing countries borrowers' participation in the Euro-bond market during the seventies was small and heavily concentrated (Mexico and Brazil being the main participators). The share of developing countries in the Euro-bond market fell to 6 per cent in 1981, and declined even further in 1982 (Johnson, 1982). However, because of their limited importance, concentration here will be on Euro-credits.

As shown in Table 5.3, the Euro-currency market has grown rapidly and steadily since the mid-sixties. This book makes use of statistical series published by the Bank for International Settlements (BIS); the BIS is recognised as offering the most accurate, official measurement of the Euro-currency system even though its coverage is not complete. It is necessary to point out a problem regarding these series. Even though inter-bank deposits of foreign currencies are netted out for the inner countries, many inter-bank transactions are still included. This accepted measure of the Euro-currency market is not comparable to monetary aggregates at a national level, which measures only assets held by non-banks. In fact, attempts to eliminate completely inter-bank transactions from the Euro-currency market (and thus make it comparable to national macro-economic aggregates) have necessarily failed, as the very essence of this market is linked to inter-bank transactions.

Increased Lending to Developing Countries

At the same time as the Euro-currency market expanded at a very rapid pace, the proportion of its loans going to developing countries grew very substantially reaching about 50 per cent in the late seventies. These large flows have led to an increasing 'privatisation' of the structure of the debt of developing countries.

Private multinational corporations and public borrowers of the industrial countries were the biggest users of the Euro-currency markets in the 1960s. As mentioned previously, in this period the external sources of finance for the developing countries were suppliers' credits and official flows (both bilateral and multilateral). In the late 1960s some countries – i.e. Brazil and Mexico – began to obtain large loans from multinational private banks. This trend, which became more important between 1970 and 1973, reached particularly large dimensions after 1974.

Most analysts agree that the rapid rise in Euro-currency loans to the developing countries was not so much a result of a change of conditions in these countries as of developments and changes in the Euro-currency markets themselves.

On the one hand, an increasing number of multinational banks were increasingly eager to lend to the Third World. Intense competition and the search for new borrowers seem to have been intensified by the rapid increase in the number of banks active in the Euromarkets. The Eurobanks' wish to diversify their portfolios geographically (and thus spread risks) was added to the relatively low growth in corporate credit demand from the developed countries. Very high rates of increase for commodity prices and consequent improvements in the trade balance of the countries on the periphery during the early seventies made them attractive clients for these multinational bankers. Furthermore, multinational bankers had become acquainted with some of the peripheral countries during the 1960s and early 1970s, when providing finance to the branches of their multinational corporate clients based in the periphery. The main factor in the growth of lending to developing countries was that as the credit demand of traditional clients slowed down because of the recession in industrial countries, deposits from oil exporters and other sources were growing very fast. This prompted the banks to lend to borrowers previously considered marginal.

At the same time, there were factors which made both the public and the private sector in the majority of developing countries keen to borrow. Governments were embarking on programmes of expanded public investment, which often contained a high proportion of imported capital goods, and often were not fully financed from an individual country's own resources. This was accompanied by a relative stagnation in the net flow of official development assistance. There were also in developing countries certain government attitudes tending to favour increased borrowing from private banking sources. Governments may have preferred private loans because they seemed to place far fewer restrictions on the borrower. Loans could be made effective quickly and, formally, had few strings attached as to how funds were to be employed or how the country's economy should be managed. This was perceived as contrasting with the behaviour of international lending institutions or bilateral aid donors which have traditionally applied a high degree of formal conditionality.

It has been reported that several countries in the mid-seventies (e.g. Colombia and Brazil) planned to seek independence in national economic planning and policy from the influence of bilateral and multilateral assistance institutions by obtaining large commercial credits (Wellons, 1977; Dell and Lawrence, 1980). New financial options seemed to provide an additional range of manoeuvre for governments in developing countries. Furthermore, in some developing countries reliance on foreign direct investment was reduced as governments expressed a political preference for contractor, agency or mixed enterprise arrangements with foreign companies, which generally implied an increase in the demand for private foreign loans. The preference of governments often coincided with that of the transnational corporations themselves; mainly because of their desire to minimise risk, these corporations often preferred to reduce their equity investment and increase finance by loans. Thus, governments seemed to prefer foreign private loans both to official credits and to direct investment, partly because the former were perceived as generating a lesser degree of dependence, thus allowing greater autonomy for the national government.

The forces described above determined the willingness of multinational banks to lend to developing countries, as well as these countries' willingness to borrow. The development of new operational techniques in the Euro-currency market, particularly during the late sixties, allowed a reduction in the individual risk for the Eurobanks responsible for these loans to developing countries.

Several innovations occurred which diminished risks for large loans with long maturities, that is the type of credits required by developing countries. First, the roll-over credit was created, based on a floating interest rate that varies approximately with the cost of the money to the lender, who obtains his funds on the essentially short-term interbank market. The base rate for these loans to the developing countries is often London Inter-Bank Offer Rate (LIBOR), or the US prime rate – both measures of the cost of funds to the banks. In addition to this variable base rate, a 'spread' or margin over LIBOR or the US prime rate is charged; it reflects both the liquidity in the market at the time and creditworthiness of the borrower. The cost of the credit also includes a 'management fee', and a 'commitment fee', charged on the unused portion of funds. Thus, although the loan to the developing country may have a long maturity (i.e. ten years), the interest rate is changed every time the credit is rolled-over (usually every three or six months). This floating interest rate, as it is called, is crucial because it passes on to the borrower one of the most important risks of the market (it is the borrower who must bear both the cyclical and the long-term changes of the interest rates).

Secondly, a very large part of the transactions by developing countries on the Euro-currency markets has been by means of syndicated loans. Syndicated loans, which originated in the late sixties, are credits shared by a large number of Eurobanks. This mechanism has allowed the default risks of large loans to be spread over a great number of banks; it has also allowed smaller banks to participate in the Euro-currency market.

Thirdly, 'consortium banks' were developed when several multinational banks jointly set up a single institution in the market, which further reduced the limits of individual bank liability for individual loans. Some of these 'consortium banks' had the additional advantage of being specialised in lending to a particular region, and therefore having greater knowledge about it (e.g. Libra Bank for Latin America).

This was particularly useful in the initial stages of Euro-currency lending to developing countries.

Trends in Euro-currency Financing in the Seventies

The sharp fluctuations in the market show that, to a relatively large degree, the conditions (of cost and maturity) under which countries may borrow may be relatively independent of the country's 'performance' or 'creditworthiness', and depend more on the general state of the market at a specific time. This is much more true in situations when the market is extremely liquid. As explained following, the country's 'performance' or 'creditworthiness' is more important in determining the *level* of loans which it can obtain in the market. When the market is very liquid (e.g. late seventies), 'creditworthiness' becomes somewhat less important even for determining the level of loans. However, during times of tighter credit (the situation since mid-1982) a greater degree of bank discrimination towards borrowing countries becomes evident.

First, a description will be given of the general trends in Euro-currency financing to developing countries, citing as examples developments in the mid-seventies. When the developing countries first entered the Euromarkets in the early seventies, conditions were favourable to those who borrowed. Maturities were long: 82.5 per cent of the publicised Euro-currency credits in 1973-4 had a maturity of seven years or more (*The Banker*; 1977). At that time spreads were low. For prime Latin American borrowers, from 1973 to 1974, the average spread was well below 1 per cent. At the time, prime COMECON borrowers had even lower spreads (*Euromoney*, March 1978). Borrowing was extremely concentrated. In 1973 according to information based on World Bank data, 15 of the relatively higher-income developing countries owed about 85 per cent of the recorded debt to foreign banks of all non oil exporting developing countires.

A new phase of the Euro-currency market was begun after the first large increase in the price of oil at the end of 1973. The demand for Euro-currency credits by developing countries (particularly the higher-income ones) increased sharply, as those countries endeavoured to finance their large current account deficits. Supply of funds to the Euro-currency markets increased rapidly as the OPEC countries, in their search for safe investment opportunities, turned primarily to the banking systems of the United States and the United Kingdom. One of the main reasons why London and New York were the principal beneficiaries of the 'petromoney recycling' was that they were the only international money markets already large enough and with sufficient links to absorb the vast sums being deposited by the oil producers. The other main reason was that, whereas the oil surplus countries may have been willing to lend directly to safe borrowers such as the US and Germany, they wanted to interpose commercial banks as a buffer between themselves and the 'higher-risk borrowers' – the developing countries. Thus, the surplus countries shifted the risk involved in lending to developing countries to the private banks.

Initially, the private banks were unwilling to assume this role fully. The banks were concerned particularly with the very short-term nature of the deposits by the oil exporting countries, combined with the medium- and long-term demand for loans from countries wishing to finance balance of payments deficits partly as a result of the higher oil price. In the case of the developing countries, fears were exacerbated by the publicised inability of certain countries to meet their short-term obligations. Several bank failures (the main one being that of Herstatt) restricted the inter-bank Euromarket for a time.

As a result of these fears, borrowing conditions for developing countries became tighter in the Euro-currency markets. Maturities were shortened drastically; in 1974 to 1975 only 31 per cent of loans to developing countries were for seven years or more, as opposed to 82.5 per cent the year before (*The Banker*, 1977). Spreads over the London Inter-Bank Offer Rate (LIBOR) rose, as did management fees. Selectivity was applied in lending to most developing countries; Eurobanks began to scrutinise more closely the purpose of loans, debt-service ability and creditworthiness factors.

Since mid-1975, Eurobankers were feeling increasing pressure from the recession and the consequent fall in industrial country borrowing, and from the large new supplies of domestic and international funds. Even though they became more eager to lend to developing countries, borrowing conditions remained severe.

By 1976, conditions prevailing in the international financial markets were in some respects those of a borrowers' market. However, according to the Bank for International Settlements (1977), because most of the demand came from countries with a weak payments balance and high levels of foreign indebtedness, there was a shortage of 'first class borrowers'. As a result, there was sharp competition to accommodate such borrowers, and conditions for them improved quite rapidly throughout 1976. On the other hand, conditions for developing countries improved only very slightly. According to the same bank (*Annual Report*, 1977) in 1976 borrowers in countries with 'a high level of foreign indebtedness and little prospect of an improvement in their payments balances, found it increasingly difficult to obtain financial accommodation in the international markets and were, if anything, subject to tougher loan conditions than in 1975'.

According to a report published by the US Department of Commerce (Seiber, 1977), towards the end of 1976 the market had clearly become a 'borrowers' market'. This report quotes a rather poetic banker who said that 'the Eurobankers were returning with the swallows to the finance of developing countries'. It is interesting that the same US Department of Commerce report says that (towards the end of 1976), 'names that had been unacceptable are returning to the market – Chile, Yugoslavia, Fiji, the Cameroons'.

Different analysts agree about the trends prevalent in 1977. According to the 1978 Bank for International Settlements *Report*, in 1977 'under the impact of the liquidity-creating effects of the US external payments deficit, the market has become increasingly supply-determined'. In fact, this report is concerned about the degree to which lending margins have been squeezed, which can 'hardly be considered in the interest of the stability of the market as a whole'. Furthermore, 'even the margins asked of some borrowing countries of lower credit standing declined in 1977 to levels that can hardly have left very much room for the banks to build up adequate reserves against losses'. Moreover, the list of eligible borrowers and borrowing countries had tended to lengthen, as had maturities, and also the average size of individual loans had risen again.

Thus, during 1977, 72 per cent of loans to developing countries had a maturity of five years or more (as opposed to 35 per cent in 1976) (World Bank, 1978). This process continued into 1978, with the financial institutions and publications expressing increasing concern about the extremely favourable conditions to borrowers (see, for example, several articles in *Euromoney*, October 1978). Average maturities continued to rise, the fall in spreads over LIBOR became increasingly generalised to borrowers of different credit standings. (This contrasts with the 1976 situation, when conditions improved mainly for prime borrowers.)

It is interesting that for a short period, non oil developing countries became net suppliers of funds to the Euro-currency market. Not only did new lending to non oil developing countries, by banks in the Group of Ten countries and Switzerland and the offshore branches of US banks, fall from nearly $18 billion in 1976 to $11.3 billion in 1977; new deposits in 1977 received from developing countries by these banks equalled $12.9 billion. As a result, the non oil developing countries, that had borrowed a net amount of nearly $30 billion in the three years frm 1974 to 1976, became net suppliers of new funds to the banks in the international markets, to the extent of $1.6 billion in 1977 (Bank for International Settlements, 1978).

The process described above is explained by the fact that in 1977 borrowing from private multinational banks – particularly by non oil developing countries – was not solely dependent on current balance of payments financing requirements. In fact, there was much borrowing to increase foreign exchange reserves, either to replace the sharp falls in previous years or to obtain a larger cushion of reserves than the countries had had previously. It is interesting that practically all these reserve increases were deposited in the 'reporting banks'[2] – as defined above. Thus, the $25.7 billion total of new deposits received by the reporting banks from non oil developing countries during 1976 and 1977 compares very closely with a simultaneous increase of US$20.3 billion in these countries' official foreign exchange holdings. Naturally, the improvement in balance of payments and reserve positions of many of these countries has been an important factor in whetting the banks' appetite for further lending.

During 1978 and most of 1979, conditions for all borrowing countries (including developing ones) continued to improve. This was reflected in a decline of the *Euromoney Index* (which is essentially a weighted average spread divided by a weighted average maturity). For upper middle developing countries, terms deteriorated during 1980, were relatively constant in 1981 and have worsened substantially again since early 1982. For smaller debtors (see IMF, 1982c) spreads still declined in 1981, even though maturities were shortening; for them also, conditions deteriorated in 1982. Over the last few years, there has been a considerable narrowing in the differential between larger, richer country debtors and poorer, small country debtors (this has occurred mainly since 1977 and early 1978).

'Creditworthiness' criteria

It is necessary to examine briefly the criteria of 'creditworthiness' or 'performance' applied by multinational banks to the developing countries. These criteria are important partly because they determine differentials in conditions (of cost and maturity) granted to different borrowers at a particular time and mainly, because they allow individual banks to fix quantitative limits of maximum lending to individual countries, often called country exposure or country limits.

The task of quantifying the elements which determine a bank's assessment of a country's creditworthiness seems an almost impossible one. It is still relatively difficult to obtain reliable and complete data on the magnitude of Euro-currency finance going from specific banks to specific countries. Furthermore, given the confidential nature of the transactions involved, international bankers are somewhat reluctant to reveal the exact factors that determine finance to individual countries – even though there is an increasing volume of literature published by banks and bankers related to this subject. Even when bankers wish to quantify precisely the elements which determine a country's creditworthiness, subjectivity (or 'gut feel' as the bankers call it) inevitably plays a major role. This subjectivity was expressed by Walter Wriston, Chairman of First National City Bank, when he said that 'in the last analysis credit is not numbers. It's people. So in the management of a country, as in that of a company, the determinative force is the ability of a government to react to circumstances' (*The Banker*, 1974).

Finally, the behaviour of individual banks varies substantially, according to their size, country of origin and other factors. For this, econometric studies (for example, Kapur, 1977) on the subject, although interesting, seem to be of limited usefulness, offering only very broad indicators of the variables determining banks' evaluation of a country's creditworthiness. A few general conclusions can be deduced from these empirical analyses, as well as from the documents produced by the bankers themselves.

'Creditworthiness' is commonly defined as the bank's perception of the country's ability and willingness to meet future interest and principal payments on the loan. The type of evaluation is naturally derived from the traditional functions of commercial banking. When lending to countries, in the same way as when making loans to enterprises, banks stress the financial and short-term criteria. Because they are basically interested in the country's ability to pay back its loan, in foreign exchange, they particularly emphasise balance of payments analysis and availability of foreign exchange reserves.

The great emphasis on foreign exchange availability and flows is reflected very clearly in the literature on creditworthiness analysis (see, several articles in *Euromoney* and also O'Brien, 1981), it has also been confirmed in personal interviews with bankers themselves. Perhaps it is expressed most clearly and logically in a speech by H.D. Schuler, Director of International Operations Division, in the US Comptroller of the Currency Office. Schuler's views have a large and increasing influence, as the role of the Comptroller of the Currency in evaluating foreign lending by United States banks is growing:

> The Committee (formed by officers from his department) first looks to external economic information; e.g. balance of payments trends over the last few years, the expected results for the next twelve months (the short-term) and the external debt structure as well as the service requirements for the same period. Secondly, the Committee's evaluation of medium and long-term loans places greater emphasis on the social, political effects of prevailing economic trends, and their impact on prospective cash flows for external debt service (Schuler, 1977).

General economic trends and policies of a country are also evaluated by the bankers from the perspective of their impact on financial variables, with a strong emphasis on balance of payments. The quality of a country's economic management is associated with factors such as 'the relative strength of its central bank and/or finance ministry'. The promptness of current account adjustment in response to higher oil prices and world recession has been a good test of the quality of the economic teams throughout the world. Competent and appropriate policies also assure good relationships with the International Monetary Fund and the World Bank.

In fact, the private multinational banks have increasingly linked their evaluation of a country's 'creditworthiness' to its 'good relations with the IMF'. As the International Monetary Fund also gives priority to financial (and particularly balance of payments) equilibrium, and has both experience and direct leverage to impose such priorities on individual countries, multinational banks have increasingly linked or even conditioned their loans to a country's previous signing of a stand-by agreement with the IMF and/or compliance with its performance clauses. Although these parallel operations have been taking place for a long time, now they are becoming increasingly widespread. In fact, many countries seek stand-by arrangements with the IMF, mainly or exclusively so that, once given 'this certificate of good behaviour', they can obtain credits from the private multinational banks or renegotiate existing loans. The very intimate link between IMF and private bank lending (as well as rescheduling) is well illustrated by the experience of Mexico in late 1982.

Another element which has a marked effect upon the evaluation of a country's creditworthiness is the size of a country's *per capita* Gross Domestic Product, as well as its recent growth record. Although in the past years there has been an excessive liquidity in the market allowing even poor countries with low growth rates to enter, their participation is still very small. Furthermore, the total outstanding net debt of the non oil developing countries to the multinational banks is still very concentrated in a few countries. These countries either have relatively higher *per capita* GDP, their GDP *per capita* is growing rapidly, or they fulfil both conditions. As a result, four developing countries (Mexico, Brazil, South Korea and the Philippines) – the largest borrowers – accounted for over 50 per cent of total accumulated debt to international banks in December 1980 (Bank for International Settlements, 1981b). The 1981 OECD *Development Cooperation Review* estimated that low-income countries obtained only *2.6 per cent* of total net lending to oil importing developing countries during the period 1972-80. A large number of developing countries, particularly the poorest ones, are not considered 'creditworthy' by the private bankers; these countries not only have very little access to private lending but are in many cases even net creditors of the international banks, as their reserves deposited with those banks exceed the loans received. Most of the poorest countries which are net creditors to the private international banks are in Africa or Asia; however, countries such as Haiti, Guatemala, Paraguay and Surinam in Latin America are also in this category (Bank for International Settlements, 1981b).

Here an important difference in the implication of private and official flows arises. A much higher proportion of public funds goes to the poorer LDCs. Thus, the swing towards private flows favoured access to external finance by the middle-income LDCs, and relatively worsened the access of the poorest countries to international finance. As a result, the 'privatisation' of financial flows seems to have contributed towards greater inequality amongst developing countries.

In the seventies the poorest countries were unable to follow the example of the middle-income countries and finance their increased balance of payments deficits by additional external flows; as a result their capacity to import declined. As the World Bank 1981 *World Development Report* indicates, during the seventies growth in GDP *per capita* for the poorest countries declined substantially as compared with their position in the sixties; most disturbing in this respect was the evolution in the poorest countries of Sub-Saharan Africa, where average

GDP *per capita* actually declined by 0.4 per cent annually during the seventies. Whereas many factors may have contributed to this unsatisfactory development, constraints on their capacity to import played a major role, and greater external finance would have helped them achieve a better performance.

In the same way as direct investment and official flows, multinational bank lending on a large scale was initiated mainly by US institutions. After initial dominance by US banks, private lending has been increasingly 'transnationalised'. This trend became much more marked towards the end of the seventies; whereas in December 1977 US banks accounted for about 50 per cent of total outstanding claims on all LDCs, the share of US banks' lending between December 1977 and June 1979 was less than 10 per cent (Bacha and Diaz-Alejandro, 1981). As lending by US banks to the LDCs started to grow much more slowly (mainly because US banks were concerned at the high level of their LDC exposure), the initiative was taken by West European, Japanese and OPEC banks.

As discussed above, in Latin America in the sixties net official inflows financed net outflows of foreign direct investment – the reason being that the latter flows were higher than the former. In the seventies an important proportion of total private bank lending serviced payments of profit remittances by foreign investors, interest and amortisation of official debt and, increasingly, the private credits themselves. As shown in Table 5.4 the category of foreign investments' profits remained relatively constant as a proportion of exports of goods and services while both interest payments and amortisation soared, particularly since the mid-seventies. This latter trend results from the 'privatisation' of the debt (which leads to shorter average maturities and an increase in the proportion of credits serviced on variable commercial interest rates), as well as the dramatic rise in Euromarket interest rates since 1979.

The Cost of Private Lending

Therefore, a problematic aspect of commercial lending to developing countries is that the conditions of the loans are less favourable than those of other sources of finance (i.e. ODA loans and export credits). On average, maturities for private loans are shorter than those for official loans. Of greater importance is that the cost of borrowing privately (particularly by means of the syndicated roll-over loans, which have characterised Euromarket lending to developing countries), has been on average higher than the official flows; perhaps even more problematic is the variability of the interest rate paid on contracted loans, which changes every three to six months following the fluctuations of interest rates in the main industrial countries (and particularly the US). This variability adds an important element of uncertainty to developing countries' attempts to predict and plan their future balance of payments flows.

As a result of rapid increases in interest rates of industrial countries since 1979, the gap between interest paid on commercial loans with floating interest and that paid on fixed interest debt has increased substantially.

Table 5.4: Net Financial Service Charges of Latin America, excluding Oil Exporters, relative to Exports of Goods and Services (percentages)

Period	Interests[a]	Profits[b]	Amortisation[c]	Capital Service Ratio[d]
1950-4	1.3	5.9	2.8	10.0
1955-9	2.3	5.2	7.2	14.7
1960-4	4.0	6.5	10.9	21.4
1965-9	5.5	8.8	13.7	27.0
1970-3	7.4	7.1	17.2	31.9
1974-6	11.1	5.5	19.1	35.7
1977-9	12.0	6.8	28.1	47.0[e]

Notes: a. Refers to net interest and profits (subtracting those received by Latin American residents). b. This category overestimates the impact on balance of payments, as it includes earning of foreign direct investment, whether remitted abroad or reinvested domestically. c. Amortisations cover those for both private and public debt of more than one year. d. Capital service ratio adds the three former columns. The debt-service ratio would add the first and the third columns. e. Only 1977-8.
Source: Bacha and Diaz-Alejandro (1981), based on ECLA data.

As can be seen in Table 5.5, the floating interest costs of developing countries more than doubled from *8.2 per cent* of their outstanding debt in 1971-3 to an estimated *18.0 per cent* in 1981. As an effect of rising interest rates and of the increasing 'privatisation' of financial flows (which implied a higher proportion of floating rate debts) the cost of servicing interests has risen rapidly for LDCs, both as a proportion of total debt (see Table 5.5) and as a proportion of total exports of goods and services (see Table 5.6). Fortunately, in this case the low-income countries were much less seriously affected than the others, as they borrow so little on the private markets (see Table 5.6).

As the OECD makes clear in its 1981 *Development Cooperation Review* the most seriously affected by these trends were Brazil and Mexico, whose gross and, particularly, net borrowing in variable interest loans (the latter equal to loans minus deposits) was such a high proportion of the total.

The increase in debt-service liabilities has been so steep that the *net transfer of resources to developing countries* (which is the proportion of borrowed funds available for buying imports and increasing reserves, after amortisation and interest payments) declined sharply as a proportion of gross borrowing, *from 50 per cent in 1975-6 to 22 per cent in 1980*.

1970	1975-6	1978	1980
43%	50%	40%	22%

(World Bank, *World Development Report*, 1981.)

Table 5.5: Interest Cost to Oil Importing Developing Countries, of their Outstanding Debts (average annual percentage rate)

	1971-3	1974-8	1979	1980	1981
Fixed interest[a]	4.0	4.4	4.9	5.0	5.2
Floating interest[b]	8.2	9.3	12.3	15.3	18.0
Total	4.8	5.9	7.2	8.4	9.5

Notes: a. Interest payments during the year as percentage of total outstanding debt, all expressed in US$. b. Estimated total cost, including spreads and fees.
Source: *OECD Development Cooperation Review 1981.*

Table 5.6: Interest Payments as Percentage of Exports of Goods and Services

	1973	1975	1977	1978	1979	1980	1981
Interest payment ratio							
All non oil LDCs	4.4	4.8	4.6	5.5	6.5	7.4	7.2
Low-income LDCs	3.1	2.8	2.7	3.0	3.0	3.2	3.4

Source: IMF *World Economic Outlook 1981*, Table 30.

Official Flows in the Seventies

Even though official flows to developing countries increased less than the total capital flows to the Third World, it should be stressed that they did grow significantly. As can be seen in Table 5.7, within official flows 'multilateral loans' was the item which grew most rapidly during the seventies (by 9.9 per cent in real terms) followed by official development assistance and official export credits (which grew by 7.5 per cent and 7.2 per cent respectively).

Table 5.7: Oil Importing Developing Countries: Financing Current Deficits, 1970-80

	Level (current prices)		Annual Percentage Growth (constant prices)
	1970	1980	1970-80
Current account balance	-8.6	-69.6	12.1
Financed by			
1. Net capital flows	9.1	55.3	9.0
a. Total aid (grants and concessional loans)	3.1	16.3	7.5
b. Medium- and long-term borrowing	4.3	33.4	16.6
Official export credits	0.5	2.6	7.2
Multilateral	0.5	3.2	9.4
Private	3.4	27.5	19.7
c. Private direct investment	1.7	5.6	2.7
2. Change in reserves and short-term borrowing	0.5	14.3	

Source: World Bank, ***World Development Report 1981***, Table 5-3.

As the 1981 *World Development Report* highlights, the evolution of official flows was much more satisfactory in the first half of the seventies, when aid grew quite rapidly, largely as a result of the sharp increase in OPEC aid (see Table 5.8). OPEC aid rose to US$5.5 billion in 1975 which equalled 27 per cent of total aid and 2.94 per cent of OPEC GNP, as compared with Development Assistance Committee (DAC) aid which reached only 0.34 per cent of DAC GNP in 1975 (see Table 5.9). An important feature of OPEC financial assistance to developing countries is the high proportion of it granted on conces-

Table 5.8: Total Net Resource Receipts of Developing Countries from all Sources

Net disbursements	1970	1971	1972	1973	1974	1975	1976	1977	1978	1979	1980 ($ billion)
Official Development Assistance	8.05	9.29	9.88	11.62	15.33	19.33	19.02	20.16	23.75	28.91	33.46
I. Bilateral											
a. DAC countries	5.66	6.33	6.63	7.09	8.23	9.81	9.50	10.08	13.12	15.91	17.64
b. OPEC countries	0.36	0.37	0.48	1.22	3.02	4.92	4.54	3.94	3.25	4.93	6.11
c. CMEA countries	0.96	1.26	1.38	1.35	1.26	0.73	1.05	1.09	1.28	1.75	1.80
d. Other countries	–	–	–	–	–	0.03	0.06	0.08	0.10	0.12	0.20
2. Multilateral agencies	1.07	1.33	1.39	1.96	2.82	3.84	3.87	4.97	6.00	6.20	(7.71)
of which: OPEC financed	–	–	–	–	0.12	0.16	0.42	1.23	0.96	0.26	0.26
Non-concessional flows	10.92	11.80	13.29	19.75	19.71	34.34	38.57	43.39	56.08	54.95	55.49
1. Bilateral											
a. Direct investment	3.69	3.31	4.23	4.72	1.89	11.51	8.64	9.59	11.83	13.62	9.69
b. Bank sector[a]	3.00	3.30	4.80	9.70	10.00	12.00	15.00	15.50	22.87	19.67	(18.00)
c. Bond lending	0.30	0.30	0.52	0.58	0.28	0.42	1.22	3.20	2.67	1.14	(2.00)
d. Private export credits	2.09	2.71	1.44	1.15	2.40	4.42	7.22	9.11	10.22	9.49	12.20
e. Official export credits	0.59	0.71	0.75	1.18	0.86	1.22	1.39	1.48	2.15	1.72	2.46
f. DAC other official	0.15	0.28	0.43	0.90	0.65	0.56	0.57	0.48	1.27	0.95	2.24
g. OPEC countries[b]	0.20	0.19	–	0.14	0.92	1.50	1.61	0.89	(1.01)	(1.00)	(1.00)
h. Other countries[c]	0.10	–	–	–	0.79	0.04	0.12	0.09	0.87	(3.20)	(3.10)
i. CMEA countries	0.11	0.10	0.11	0.10	0.09	0.09	0.12	0.11	0.10	–	–
2. Multilateral	0.69	0.90	1.01	1.28	1.83	2.58	2.68	2.94	3.09	4.16	(4.80)
of which OPEC financed	–	–	–	–	0.02	0.06	0.13	0.27	0.16	0.22	0.14
Total receipts	18.97	21.09	23.17	31.37	35.04	53.67	57.59	63.35	79.33	(83.86)	(88.95)
Memorandum items:											
Private sector grants[d]	0.86	0.91	1.04	1.37	1.22	1.34	1.35	1.49	1.65	1.95	2.31
IMF Purchases, net[e]	0.34	0.05	0.30	0.36	1.74	3.24	2.98	- 0.43	- 0.93	–	2.61
IMF Trust Fund (included under ODA 2 above)	–	–	–	–	–	–	–	0.18	0.86	0.68	1.64

Notes: a. Excluding (i) bond lending and (ii) export credits extended by banks which are included under private export credits. Includes loans by branches of OECD banks located in offshore centres, and for 1980 participation of non OECD banks in international syndicates. b. Official flows only: no information is available on private flows. c. Includes Ireland, Luxembourg, Spain, Yugoslavia, India, Israel. d. Drawings minus repayments including reserve tranches (amounting to $103 million in 1979 and $309 million in 1980) but excluding loans by the IMF Trust Fund included under multilateral ODA above. Note: Figures concerning non-DAC member countries are based as far as possible on information released by donor countries and international organisations, and completed by OECD Secretariat estimates based on other published and unpublished sources. It has therefore not been possible fully to verify that they comply in all respects with the norms and criteria used by DAC members in their statistical reports made directly to the OECD Secretariat.
Source: OECD Development Co-operation (1981).

sional terms.

In the first half of the 1970s, official development assistance received by low-income countries increased significantly, growing in real terms by 60 per cent between 1973 and 1975.

In the second half of the 1970s, official flows – and particularly concessional flows through ODA – grew slowly; of particular concern was that *in the case of low-income oil importers, official flows actually declined in real terms*. This is particularly serious, since low-income countries rely to such an extent on concessional flows to meet their increased deficits. (In 1979 ODA reached 81 per cent of total finance for the low-income countries, while representing only 42 per cent for the middle-income countries and 2 per cent for the NICs).

Table 5.9: Comparative ODA Performance of Major Donor Groups

		ODA $ million	
	1975	1978	1979
DAC[a]	13022	18794	20876
OPEC	5517	4338	5197
CMEA[b]	1437	1266	1852
	266	224	560
		ODA as % of GNP	
	1975	1978	1979
DAC[a]	0.34	0.33	0.32
OPEC	2.94	1.38	1.44
CMEA[b]	0.13	0.09	0.11
	0.02	0.02	0.03
		% of Total ODA	
	1975	1978	1979
DAC[a]	65	77	75
OPEC	27	18	18
CMEA[b]	8	5	7

Notes: a. Refers to the members of the Development Assistance Committee of the OECD. b. The first row includes aid to Cuba, Democratic People's Republic of Korea and Vietnam. The second row excludes aid to those three countries.
Source: UNCTAD (1983), based on data in ***OECD Development Co-operation: 1980 Review*** (Paris, 1980).

By 1979 ODA from OECD countries was little higher as a proportion of GNP than it had been in 1975, and only about half of the 0.70 per cent of GNP which most of them had accepted as a target. Their collective performance was heavily influenced by the record of the largest donor, the US, whose aid was a mere 0.27 per cent of GNP in

1980. The share of non-OECD countries in total ODA increased during the 1970s, but reached its peak in 1975. Most of this came from capital surplus oil exporters. As oil surpluses declined, OPEC's share in total ODA declined to 18 per cent in 1979, but rose to 20 per cent in 1980. In 1980, OPEC countries were contributing about 1.40 per cent of their GNP to aid, while capital surplus oil exporters were contributing 3.1 per cent of their GNP to aid.

Notes

1. Even though part of this increase reflects US inflation, the growth in real terms of net private flows is really dramatic.
2. See, for example, sources with such different analytical frameworks as the US Congress Committee on Foreign Relations (1977); R.I. McKinnon (1977) and Aronson (1977).

6 THE ROLE OF THE INTERNATIONAL MONETARY FUND

As essay by Susan Strange points out that Fund lending has tended to follow a selective pattern:

> a policy was slowly hammered out, which applied the Fund's resources in a highly political manner. Without its ever being stated in so many words, the Fund's operational decisions made its resources available neither to those in the greatest needs nor to those with the best record of good behaviour in keeping to the rules, but paradoxically to those members whose financial difficulties were most likely to jeopardise the stability of the international monetary system (Strange, 1973:277).

Latin America was till the late seventies not a significant borrower of Fund resources. The net contribution of Fund credit for current account deficit has been relatively very small, and occasionally even negative (see the item of compensatory finance in Table 4.2).

Graph 1 shows that the increases in the level of use of Fund credit since the sixties were much smaller for the Western Hemisphere than for other non oil exporting developing countries and for industrial countries. During the seventies net Fund credit to the Western Hemisphere was significant only during the period 1975-6, when the Oil Facility (which operated only during those two years to compensate for the rise in the price of oil) and the Compensatory Financing Facility (which compensates for slower growth in exports than the trend value) were widely used by Latin American countries.

Even when the net credit contribution of the Fund to Latin America has been quantitatively small, its impact on economic policies has been significant. In fact, the practice of attaching economic policy conditions and performance criteria to the provision of Fund loans was gradually developed in the 1950s, *mainly using Latin American economies* as testing grounds for such techniques (Thorp and Whitehead, 1979: 3). Furthermore, the critique of Fund conditionality and of the monetarist models implicit in the Fund's recommendations, began in Latin America in the mid-fifties; it was one of the main origins of the Latin American 'structuralist' school on inflation, which became widely

Graph 1: Net Annual Usage of Fund Credit (in billions of SDRs)

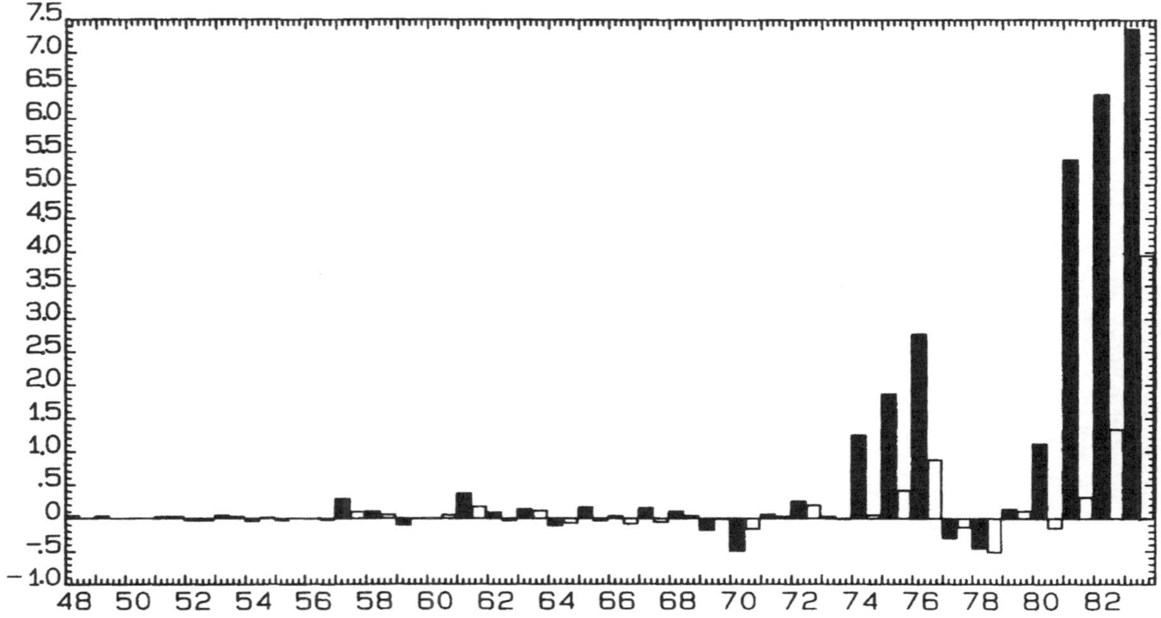

Non-Oil Developing Countries = ■ ;*Western Hemisphere* = □
Source : IMF International Financial Statistics

(Graph by Robert Griffith-Jones)

known throughout the rest of the world.

Access to Fund credit, particularly in the upper credit tranches, which implies stringent acceptance of Fund conditionality, usually has acted as a catalyst for increased inflows from other sources. In the sixties, US aid programmes were often conditional on the previous signing of an IMF stand-by agreement by the recipient country. This type of linkage was very common in the sixties in Latin America when disbursements of US AID loans were frequently dependent upon the fulfilment of narrowly defined fiscal, monetary and exchange rate targets previously determined in a stand-by agreement with the Fund; this was clearly illustrated by American aid to Chile in 1963-6 (Griffith-Jones, 1979: 433). Similarly in the seventies, private banks frequently made it a precondition for granting a credit that the country should previously have agreed a 'stabilisation' programme with the IMF.

The role of the IMF is also crucial in the process of debt renegotiation, both public and private. The role of the IMF in attracting new loans or helping to renegotiate existing ones has been dramatically strengthened since late 1982. As stated in the main article in *Euromoney* (January 1983: 35) 'There has never been a tighter collaboration between the Fund, the governments, the central banks of the industrial countries and the commercial banks . . . There has never been a situation in the past where the managing director (of the IMF) has told the banks to lend . . . and told them how much.'

Fund leverage to exercise influence on countries' policies and developments seems to be greater when there are few alternative sources of finance available, e.g. Jamaica 1978-9. This was the general case in the fifties when alternatives to IMF finance hardly existed at all as both private and other multilateral official credit flows were at a very low level. The situation that existed in the fifties is becoming increasingly more common in the eighties as private banks become more reluctant to provide additional finance to developing countries. Fund leverage is also in evidence when alternative finance exists, but those who can grant it are unwilling to lend to a particular country or will lend to it only if the Fund does so previously (e.g. in the case of Peru in 1978 and Brazil, Mexico and Argentina in 1982 and 1983).

The influence which the International Monetary Fund can exercise seems to be least when a developing country either has little need for external finance (e.g. major coffee exporters during large price rises of coffee a few years ago) or can easily obtain external finance without IMF conditionality as a precondition. This has been best illustrated in Latin America by Brazil during the seventies, which was able to avoid

Fund credit in the upper tranches, and thus to preserve greater autonomy in economic policy-making. Brazil managed to obtain sufficient credit during the seventies from the Euromarkets because of her 'creditworthiness'. However, this situation changed when private bankers were able to exercise sufficient pressure for Brazil to be 'forced' to go to the Fund.

Different types of IMF lending facilities with different levels of conditionality attached have been referred to here; for clarification these will be described briefly following (see also, for example, Daniel, 1981: 29-31). Currently, the only completely unconditional facility is the reserve tranche (i.e. purchase of a member's *own* quota subscription to the Fund) which is, in any case, part of a country's foreign exchange reserves. The facilities of low conditionality are not uniform in their terms. Under the buffer stock facility and the first 50 per cent of drawings under the compensatory financing facility (which compensates for temporary declines of a country's export earnings in relation to their recent trend), there is virtually no conditionality once a balance of payments need has been demonstrated. For the second 50 per cent of drawings under the latter facility, a country must be 'co-operating' with the Fund to solve its balance of payments difficulties. First credit tranche programmes are still of low conditionality in the sense that drawings are not normally conditional on performance, but they do contain objectives and performance targets which the borrower is expected to fulfil.

The stand-by arrangement and the extended Fund facility (EFF) in the upper credit tranche involve programmes of full conditionality, ***with access to periodic drawings*** – usually quarterly – dependent ***upon strict fulfilment of agreed performance criteria***. The stand-by arrangement is normally agreed for one year. The EFF (introduced in 1974) envisages a three-year programme of lending and adjustment; currently it has a ten-year repayment period. It is important to stress that, as the Fund's Managing Director stated in 1981 (IMF, 1981a: 152):

> in the period following the first wave of oil price increases approximately two-thirds of the resources were made available on terms involving a low degree of conditionality. At present (1981), by contrast, some three-quarters of our new lending commitments involve 'upper credit tranche' programmes, that is, they require rigorous adjustment policies.

The problems raised by IMF conditionality are being increasingly discussed (for valuable contributions from different perspectives, see, for example, Buira, 1981; Brett, 1979; Dell and Lawrence, 1980). We shall briefly outline here only the main issues. A general criticism is that the Fund's influence over the economic policies of member countries is concentrated on the deficit countries; this tends to impose a *deflationary bias* on the world economy as a whole, and in particular on those countries which need Fund assistance and/or its 'certificate of good behaviour' for obtaining other sources of finance.

Furthermore, the IMF has been criticised for laying too much emphasis on *rapid moves towards balance in the external sector*, at the cost of other important development objectives, such as investment and growth. The Fund has also been criticised for failing to differentiate between the causes of balance of payments disequilibria, thus failing to address changes in its criteria that might contribute to successful adjustment in the new international environment. Furthermore, even though the Fund claims that its recommendations are neutral as regards the burden of adjustment, its stress on measures such as reductions of state subsidies (which often subsidise staple foods consumed primarily by the poor), seem often to have negative effects on income distribution. Finally, the Fund admits to having a marked preference for 'market mechanisms' and unrestricted flows of foreign investment, and a dislike for direct policy tools such as price controls and restrictions on foreign exchange and trade.

The Fund has responded in some measure to all its critics. In March 1979 (IMF *Survey*, 19 March 1979) it revised its guidelines on conditionality, stressing the need to 'take into account countries' domestic, social and political objectives'. The relative relaxation or toughening of IMF conditionality is not, however, a product of official declarations on the subject, but depends both on the position of its members who are represented on the Executive Board, and that of the industrial countries' member governments. The Fund has also since the mid-seventies increased the period in which its loans reach maturity.

7 EFFECTS OF CHANGES IN THE MAGNITUDE AND COMPOSITION OF FINANCIAL FLOWS ON NATIONAL DEVELOPMENT

As the pattern of external financial flows to Latin America was modified, and as the volume of flows increased substantially, the impact which the changing and growing integration of Latin American economies into the world financial system had on those countries' economic policies and development posed very important questions. To what extent did larger financial flows (and their growing 'privatisation') augment the options open to Latin American countries in the seventies, and to what extent did they place new constraints on policy-making and on the nature of development? Did the relative degree of autonomy available to the national governments on the whole tend to increase or decrease during the seventies? How will the changes in the international flows affect countries' autonomy in the eighties?

Insufficient analysis has been carried out until now on the impact of rapidly changing financial flows on national development. However, an attempt will be made here to give some preliminary comments on this subject, looked at mainly from the perspective of the type of conditionality attached to different types of financial flows. As the analysis refers mainly to Latin America in general, less emphasis will be placed here on the specific national characteristics (political, social and economic), although these greatly influence the ultimate impact that external factors (including finance) have on national development.

Before analysing the impact of international financial flows on national development, it is necessary to clarify whether all countries are thus affected. Is 'financial dependency' a valid concept for a particular category of country? Does it refer only to developing countries? Does it apply to all developing countries? The answers seem to be found not in theoretical considerations, but in the realities of the international political and financial systems.

The reserve currency countries, particularly the United States after the Second World War, are able to finance their deficits with additional issues of their own currency; therefore they do not need to resort to institutions outside their own country for additional finance.

Similarly, countries with large and relatively permanent surpluses in their balance of payments do not require external finance; on the contrary, they provide loans and aid to other countries and to international financial institutions. Although, in theory, the Fund has power to influence policies of countries with balance of payments' surpluses (via the so-called 'scarce currency' clause) this clause has, in practice, never been invoked since the IMF was established. As a result, the Fund only exacts adjustment from countries with deficits which ask it for assistance, thus introducing a deflationary bias in the world economy. This second category of surplus countries has in the past included industrial countries such as Japan and West Germany. Particularly since late 1973, it has also included some developing countries, the oil exporting countries with low absorptive capacity; Saudi Arabia and Kuwait are the two main examples.

Both categories of countries, the reserve currency country and the surplus country, may be considered basically as being *financially independent* within the existing system.

Countries with large balance of payments deficits are not all equally 'dependent' on their financiers. Affluent countries have recourse to a diversity of sources. Thus, industrial countries, when in deficit, have access to special 'swap arrangements' amongst the Group of Ten or within the European Monetary System. This enables them to finance their deficits through credits from Central Banks of other industrial countries without adhering to any explicit conditionality. Furthermore, they have easy access to private capital markets or even direct loans from oil exporters, e.g. Saudi loans to West Germany and France. Rarely do industrial countries go to the IMF. The last occasion in recent history was the UK in 1977.

The relatively higher-income or semi-industrialised countries, had access to Euro-loans to finance their balance of payments deficits, and this also temporarily allowed them in the seventies *to avoid the explicit and detailed conditionality of the IMF.* Furthermore, particular developing countries have special access to regional financial institutions with less or different conditions, e.g. the Arab Monetary Fund.

It is more often the smaller, weaker countries which have fewer options for external finance, particularly when faced with a serious balance of payments crisis. They are therefore most often subjected to loans with more rigorous conditionality. The fact that IMF conditionality in the seventies affected mainly poorer, smaller, weaker countries is not so much a criticism of the Fund, but of the intrinsic inequities of the international financial system.

It may become a feature of the eighties that most developing countries (whether low or middle income), as well as some of the smaller industrialised ones, will have to accept IMF conditionality, as their options are increasingly narrowed. However, the pressure and influence exerted on a small, low income country by the IMF will still be greater than the one it is able to exert on a large, middle income one.

It can, therefore, be concluded that particularly in certain periods, dependency is a more relevant concept for some developing countries, the poorest and weakest. Its relevance for industrial countries and large, semi-industrialised developing countries is somewhat more limited. It is also more important in particular circumstances such as acute balance of payments crises, and/or in cases where high priority is given by a government to a strategy of opening up the economy to foreign flows. Financial dependency becomes a more valid concept for a larger group of developing countries when the options available from the international financial system become more restricted.

Not only does the impact of external finance on national development vary from country to country; one must also consider the different form that financial flows take over a period of time. Many analyses may be found on the subject of foreign direct investment. Some have argued that multinational corporations contribute to a net outflow of capital, displace local production, transfer little or inappropriate technology and encourage the transnationalisation of consumption patterns. On the whole, the impact of foreign direct investment is upon particular sectors.

Official loans and aid are granted mostly for specific projects particularly in the case of multilateral agencies, such as the World Bank and the Interamerican Development Bank. Their evaluation and surveillance are mainly in technical terms, but the use of funds is also closely monitored. Resources are allocated following sectoral priorities.

Increasingly, however, official flows (particularly of bilateral agencies, such as USAID) established programme loans for general balance of payments support. Programme loans tend to concentrate on development strategies and general macro-economic conditions. The criteria are very similar – and often in fact are directly linked to – IMF criteria. As mentioned above, disbursements of AID programme loans in the sixties, which began operating in 1963, were linked to several narrowly defined fiscal, monetary and exchange rate targets, which had been determined in the previously signed stand-by agreement with the IMF. Thus, aid through programme loans basically reinforced IMF criteria, even though also introducing others, such as structural reforms. More recently, the World Bank has introduced Structural Adjustment Loans, a form of programme lending with macro-economic conditionality.

Both in project and in programme lending, the criteria for lending are basically influenced by the governments mainly of the donor but also of the recipient countries. The allocation criteria reflect prevalent trends in development thinking in the lending agencies, which in turn respond greatly to the socio-political model they advocate. Thus, during the initial stage of the Alliance for Progress, support was given to agrarian and taxation reforms, as well as to modernisation in agriculture. Much greater stress has been placed on macro-economic and financial criteria during the late sixties and seventies; furthermore, during the seventies, great emphasis was placed on export promotion as the main vehicle for development.

The types of financial flow dominant in the seventies – private credits from multinational banks – had a rather different impact. In practice funds were hardly ever tied to specific projects, and in those cases in which they were, banks neither monitored actual expenditure nor carried out technical evaluation of the projects. Furthermore, there is no theoretical thinking on development or growth behind the lending policies of private banks. Therefore, conditionality attached to private lending is on the whole less explicit and formalised than that exercised either by multilateral or bilateral agencies. Banks seem to be less overtly political in their criteria than official institutions, as they do not serve the political interests of their country or countries so closely nor are they influenced by their parliaments, but mainly pursue profitable business. As a result, banks are on the whole willing to lend to different types of political regimes, as long as they are 'firmly established'. The banks' main criteria for lending is the profitability and security of their loans; they prefer to lend to countries from which they can obtain higher margins, and/or to those which they perceive as more clearly committed to debt repayment and more able to do so. As a result, their main emphasis is on short-term financial indicators. Great emphasis is put on variables such as the level of inflation and particularly the level of foreign exchange reserves and trade balances; it is noteworthy that the rate of investment to GDP (a rough indicator of medium-term economic prospects) is barely considered of importance as a 'creditworthiness' criterion by private banks.

It seems that initially the government of a developing country has much greater freedom to use funds in whatever manner it thinks best if it obtains private loans, rather than aid. This greater degree of freedom is severely restricted if the country faces a difficult balance of payments situation. In critical situations, the banks demand, as a precondition for granting further loans or restructuring existing ones, that the country sign a stand-by with the IMF. (This occurred, for example, in Peru during 1978 and has become very common since late 1982.) In fact excessive initial bank lending may in the medium term reinforce Fund conditionality. If a country goes to the IMF as a result of pressure from its other creditors, conditionality will be tougher and the goverment will have little bargaining power to negotiate with the Fund.

Thus, more room for manoeuvre was made possible in the seventies than existed in the sixties, particularly for the middle-income developing countries, which the banks found more 'creditworthy'. Most importantly, those developing countries that obtained such large volumes of credits on the private capital markets were able to sustain levels of imports well above those they could have afforded if such loans had not occurred. Recent studies have shown that those countries that maintained or increased their imports also maintained high growth rates of both investment and total production (Dell and Lawrence, 1980). As regards Latin America, Brazil during the seventies provides a text book example of a country which was able to continue its high growth rate through a strategy of 'debt-led growth'. Brazil's ability and willingness to borrow in order to continue importing allowed it to maintain a positive growth rate while much of the world was in recession. Finance, thus, had a counter-cyclical effect (directly on Brazil and indirectly on the rest of the world). Adjustment ceased to be the sole available option.

However, the availability of international liquidity without any technical or political surveillance may have meant that some of these foreign resources were used up in excessive increases of consumption (much of it superfluous). As the market is the main 'allocator' of these financial resources (in the industrial country and often in the recipient developing one), it may not lead to an efficient and/or a just development pattern.

Even if private credits are invested, there is the risk that unexpected changes in the international environment, such as increases in interest rates or declines in commodity prices, may mean that the foreign exchange required to service the loan will not be forthcoming in sufficient amounts or at an adequate pace. Thus, the risk of a balance of payments crisis seems greater than with official loans; and even greater still if governments exercise practically no control over private inflows and their use.

At a broader level, the wish to attract foreign private loans may encourage a policy model which overemphasises financial equilibrium to the detriment of all other aspects of economic policy. Often, the need to maintain or improve the country's 'creditworthiness' has been used to justify certain measures. One of many examples can be found in the following statement that appeared in the main Chilean newspaper, *El Mercurio* (15 October 1978).

> Chile has recently obtained from the international banking community a treatment similar to that of serious and important countries. This asset of incalculable value must be maintained at all costs, and for this it is essential to sustain an economic policy of stabilisation, which will reduce public expenditure and will moderate excessive increases in real wages.

It was also maintained in the seventies that structural changes such as 'freeing the magic of the market forces' and opening up the economy to trade and financial flows helps to improve the country's 'creditworthiness'. Certainly the large private international liquidity available has proved a powerful incentive for governments with different ideologies (including socialist ones, such as the People's Republic of China) to 'open up' their countries more to foreign credits and foreign trade.

It can be concluded that the massive explosion of private bank lending during the seventies opened new options of growth for some developing countries, in principle implying greater autonomy than aid. It is to be feared, however, that the explicit conditionality of official loans may be replaced by a less clearly perceived implicit conditionality in private loans. Furthermore, as there is practically no accountability for the use of the private credits (either in the private bank or in the borrowing country), it is possible that vast sums of money may be used for consumption of luxury goods or investment in inefficient projects. Naturally, private international credit can be channelled into productive investment, provided there is systematic effort by the borrower (either private or public) to do so.

In the next chapter, the changing nature of private lending in the early eighties and its likely impact on developing countries will be further explored.

8 THE EARLY EIGHTIES: RESCHEDULING AND THE INCREASING ROLE OF OFFICIAL INSTITUTIONS

In the early eighties, new trends emerged in the external financing of developing countries, largely as a result of the vast amount of debt already accumulated, and the prolonged recession in the industrial countries. These new trends have become much clearer since late 1982; if a precise point in time were to be identified after which these trends became more marked, the date would be the August 1982 Mexican external financial crisis. However, these problems in Mexico – followed soon after by similar problems in several of the main developing countries' debtors – were the result of economic and financial trends which had been emerging over several years.

In the context of our previous analysis, one of the most important characteristics of Latin America's external finance in the early eighties is that, unlike the previous three decades, there has not emerged a new dynamic participator to perceive rapidly increasing financial flows towards the region as best serving his own interests.

Furthermore, much of the lending which has occurred (and particularly that by the private multinational banks) has been reluctant and defensive; in fact, as the main article in *Euromoney* clearly points out 'most of the loans (in 1983) will be business the banks don't want to do' (*Euromoney*, February 1983).

The Unwilling Lenders: the Private Banks

In fact, since 1979 the growth of private bank lending to non oil developing countries had been slowing down somewhat; as a result, the share of net private long-term capital flows in the financing of these countries' current account deficits declined quite significantly. (According to the International Monetary Fund's 1982 *World Economic Outlook*, this share fell from its peak of 38.2 per cent in 1978 to 31.6 per cent in 1979 and to 27.5 per cent in 1980, even though recovering somewhat in 1981.) Although the development of international liquidity may have played an important role in this slower growth, the main factor has been the perception by the private multinational banks of increased risk to the lending country in their loans to developing countries. Furthermore, there was increasing concern in banking circles about the fact that the rates of growth of lending to developing countries since the mid-seventies had outstripped those of bank capital. Moreover, the rates of increase in loans to several countries – particularly Mexico and Argentina – were considerably above the average rate of lending, and thereby, resulted in increasing concentration of bank credit to a few countries.

It is now possible to have a relatively exact picture of the evolution of private bank lending in 1982. Even though different observers stress different aspects, it is becoming evident that slow growth of outstanding private lending to developing countries, at least in the second half of 1982, was transformed into an absolute decline of this total lending during the third quarter of 1982. Thus, BIS figures, issued in January 1983 (*BIS – International Banking Developments*, third quarter 1982) indicate that during the third quarter of 1982, banks' claims on non-OPEC developing countries actually declined by US$0.8 billion. According to these figures, during this third quarter there was still a small increase in banks' claims on Latin American countries as a whole, even though several countries' total exposure declined. (In particular that of Mexico, which fell by US$1.8 billion and that of Argentina which declined by US$0.4 billion; this was partly compensated for by the rise of banks' total claims on Brazil during this period by US$2.8 billion.) It is noteworthy that – according to BIS figures issued in April 1983, in *International Banking Developments* (fourth quarter 1982) – banks' claims on non-OPEC developing countries again increased somewhat, in the last quarter of 1982, even though at a much slower rate than in the same period in former years. This turnaround was accounted for by increased lending to countries in the Middle East, other Asian and other African countries. *Credits to Latin American countries, on the other hand, which had in the past accounted for the bulk of lending to developing countries and had still increased during the third quarter, declined in the fourth quarter by US$1 billion, the first such decrease since 1977.* Most of the lending to Latin America that did occur in the second half of 1982 was mainly involuntary, and associated with the rescheduling 'package deals'. This is in contrast with loans to Asian developing countries, to which private banks seem still very anxious to lend. The fact that spreads for Asian loans fell during 1982 becoming lower or equal to those for OECD borrowers (see Bank of England, *Quarterly Bulletin*, 1983) shows that at that time at least private banks were in fact more eager than in past years to lend to those countries. One may, as a result, see a shift in geographical distribution of private lending, not merely from lending to developing countries to a larger proportion going to industrialised countries; at the same time there may emerge a shift within lending to LDCs from lending to Latin America, to greater lending in other Third World areas, and in particular to Asian countries.

Other sources show even a sharper change for 1982, particularly for Latin America. According to *Euromoney* figures, *syndicated bank lending* to oil importing developing countries was for the whole of 1982 below 1981 levels. In particular, the *Euromoney Syndication Guide* shows *a sharp decline (of 16 per cent) in Latin America's access to syndicated lending during 1982*. In the *Euromoney* figures there is also a clear contrast between syndicated loans to Latin America during the first half of 1982, when monthly total loans often (in April, May and June) exceeded US$4 billion, and the second half of 1982 when several months showed a total below US$2 billion (the syndicated loan figures refer to gross commitments of new medium-term syndicated loans, whereas the BIS figures quoted above refer to total loan disbursements, including short term). CEPAL estimates (in *CEPAL News*, January 1983) that *total net capital inflows to Latin America fell by 55 per cent from 1981 to 1982*. A major component of these inflows, which explain this decline, was private credits.

A second characteristic of private bank lending to Latin America in recent months has been that such a high proportion of it has been to a great extent involuntary. According to the February 1983 *Euromoney* article quoted above, 'a quick poll of syndication managers suggested that they expected a maximum of 25% of all 1983 loans to be new funding, most of the other 75% will be business they don't want to do'. In fact, most of bank lending to developing countries (and particularly to Latin America) since August 1982 seems to have been either for the rescheduling of already existing debt or for new loans precisely to those countries which were rescheduling (in fact both elements were usually tied together in 'package deals' arranged after individual developing countries announced their inability to continue servicing their debts).

As the *Financial Times* stated in an editorial article on 31 January 1983 – 'International Rescheduling; the New Way with Debt' – since August 1982 such 'package deals' have been (or are being) negotiated for many of the largest developing and East European borrowers (Mexico, Argentina, Brazil, Yugoslavia, Ecuador, Romania, Chile, Cuba and Uruguay) as well as for several smaller borrowers. It has been estimated (in the February 1983 issue of Morgan Guaranty's *World Finan-*

cial Markets) that the debt of the 25 countries who were in arrears, in the process of rescheduling, or have already rescheduled portions of their debt amounts to more than US$200 billion – nearly half of the total debt LDCs and East European countries owe to commercial banks. Latin American countries are estimated to account for about 80 per cent of the bank debt of these countries.

Several of the large rescheduling packages assembled (particularly those of Mexico, Brazil and Argentina) involve private banks in quite significant increases in their lending to those countries. Thus, private banks were asked by the IMF to raise their exposure to Mexico during 1983 by 8 per cent and to Brazil by approximately 12.5 per cent. In fact, these levels of new lending by the private banks are not being determined by their own autonomous decisions. The new approach to rescheduling involves an unprecedented degree of interaction and collaboration between private banks, the IMF, the Bank for International Settlements (BIS) and the governments of industrialised countries. In particular, the IMF and the industrial countries' central banks have in several cases (Mexico and Brazil, for example) told the private banks by exactly what percentage they 'must' increase their exposure to particular countries; this degree of pressure has no precedent.

As mentioned above, in the seventies often new private bank lending to a country was conditional on it previously coming to an agreement with the IMF upon a loan. This still occurs, however, now the IMF has itself refused to agree to lend to a particular country until the private banks have committed themselves previously to making new loans for a certain sum of money. Many bankers have welcomed the IMF's moves to influence rescheduling of direct commercial credit, and to organise such 'package deals', as they perceive that this diminishes the risk of open default by particular countries. Other bankers seem to resent this new role which the IMF has assumed. For example, Mr S.M. Yassukovich, managing director of a small Euromarket bank, told the *Financial Times* on 15 December 1982 that:

> For the first time in our history as independent bankers we have been robbed of our freedom of action in taking a decision on whether to make a loan or not. We have been told that if we don't make a loan, our standing in the market could be prejudiced. It seems to be a fundamental interference with the independence of bankers. If people think through the implications of that they will

> be horrified. It is going to accelerate the process of people dropping out of the market.

The last point seems a very crucial one. Private banks (particularly but not only smaller ones, with more limited exposure in developing countries) increasingly see it as undesirable that when their loans run into difficulty, they not only have to renegotiate them but lend more to those countries, following the dictates of the IMF and their central banks. As a result, they are therefore withdrawing (either permanently or temporarily) from the syndicated and short-term loan market. For example, it has been reported (e.g. *The Times*, 1 February 1983) that as a result of IMF pressure on private banks in the Mexican 'package deal', and expecting similar pressure for Brazil, some smaller banks rapidly reduced their inter-bank credit lines to Brazil, which led to one of the most difficult financial problems for that country in the first half of 1983.

A final characteristic of recent lending and rescheduling is the difficulty and complexity of these operations. Not only do official institutions (such as the IMF, BIS and the different central banks of industrial countries) have to co-ordinate among themselves and negotiate with the government of the debtor country; all these economic actors have to reach agreement with a vast number of creditor commercial banks (which for example in the case of Mexico are reported to reach 1,400!). As a result, much time is spent by very senior representatives of developing countries in these negotiations; much of the private bankers' and senior IMF officials' time and energy is also spent in these matters. The complexity of the task also implies that agreement is delayed beyond the targeted time, and the situation is further complicated by the need for new bridging loans. For example, as a result of delays in completing the US$5 billion loan which the IMF proposed commercial banks should grant to Mexico, this country was forced to seek a bridging loan to cover its financial needs (see *Financial Times*, 16 February 1983 'Mexico Seeks Bridging Loan').

For the banks the extra time spent on these operations does have a clear financial reward. It has been reported that Mexico will have to pay almost US$200 million in fees alone for its rescheduling. Once it is in place, spreads will be significantly higher that what Mexico was paying before; as a result, it has been estimated that many banks doubled the return on assets earned from Mexico.

Causes of Countries' Inability to Repay Debts

While there has been quite detailed analysis (particularly in newspapers and banking journals) on changes in the nature of private bank rescheduling of developing country debt, until very recently much less emphasis has been placed on explaining why so many developing countries simultaneously were unable to service and repay their debts. As this problem has affected so many different countries during such a short period, it would be clearly illogical to attribute those problems largely to individual developing countries' policy mistakes. In fact, to a great extent an explanation for the erosion of developing countries ability to repay is to be found in the recent unfavourable evolution of the world economy, and in particular in the recession in industrial countries. (Naturally mistakes in national economic policies may have in some cases accentuated externally generated problems.)

The model of debt-led growth, which characterised several of the Latin American economies during the seventies, was not only viable but also quite successful while real interest rates were negative or low, and while world trade grew relatively rapidly. This situation was, however, completely transformed by the intense monetary deflation that ensued in the industrial countries. Negative real interest rates on commercial bank lending were replaced by the highest positive real interest rates ever recorded and these rates had, of course, to be paid not merely on new loans but on the accumulated old loans, contracted at variable interest rates. Furthermore, the ability to service debt without disruption of the borrowing country's economy depends on two conditions: uninterrupted world economic expansion, and access to markets of the creditor countries. Obviously, the only source from which debt can be serviced internationally is from the proceeds of exports (of goods and services) by the debtor countries. Many industrial country observers have been reluctant to admit that however responsible the borrowing country's monetary and fiscal policy is, however wisely the borrowed funds have been used, and however productive the new investment made possible by borrowing was, the capacity to repay will ultimately depend on the willingness of creditor countries to accept larger imports of goods and services from the borrowers.

Thus, the deflationary policies of the industrial countries simultaneously increased the debt-service burden of the borrowing countries – mainly because of the high nominal and real interest rates brought about by excessive reliance on monetary restrictions as a means of fighting inflation in the industrial countries – and created further problems for the borrowers by reducing demand for their imports. Particularly serious during 1982 was the collapse of primary commodity prices to their lowest levels, in real terms, in 30 years – a collapse that practically all observers agree was caused mainly by the decline of industrial country economic activity.

As a result of these trends (and the continued growth of debts), it has been estimated (in Morgan Guaranty, *World Financial Markets*, February 1983) that for the 21 major developing country borrowers from the private banks, the ratio of outstanding debt to exports of goods and services rose from 133 per cent in 1979 to 172 per cent in 1982. These countries' total debt-sevice ratio (which refers to interest on total external debt plus all maturing debt, *including amortisation of medium- and long-term debt and all short-term debt*, divided by exports of goods and services) increased from 50 per cent in 1979 to 75 per cent in 1982. *The figures estimated for the major Latin American borrowers* (which include Argentina, Brazil, Chile, Colombia, Ecuador, Mexico, Peru and Venezuela) are significantly higher and reflect even more rapid increase; in particular, the *debt-service ratio for those major Latin American borrowers rose from 76 per cent in 1979 to 125 per cent in 1982*.

Finally, the growing inability of so many countries to repay their debts and the obvious need to reschedule them (with the threat of a possible default lurking in the background) has discouraged new bank loans to those and other (e.g. neighbouring) developing countries. Thus, the financial crises were in some cases made worse – or even precipitated – by the self-fulfilling fears of private bankers and their unwillingness to lend to particular countries. These trends would have doubtlessly become much more marked had not the IMF, BIS and central banks stepped in with their 'package deals'.

The Increased Role of the IMF in Lending to Developing Countries

As mentioned previously, the IMF has since late 1982 played a very key role in the process of organising lending and rescheduling 'package deals' for developing countries. This new role has been accompanied (as well as strengthened) by the increased lending which the Fund itself has made to developing countries from the beginning of this decade until mid-1983 (which contrasts with its small contribution during the last decade). In 1978, net use of Fund resources by non oil developing countries had in fact been negative; in 1979 it had increased very marginally, by SDR0.1 billion (one SDR is equal to approximately US$1.1); however in 1980 and 1981 net use of Fund resources by developing countries increased significantly, by SDR 2.7 billion in the former year and by SDR 5.5 billion in 1981 (figures based on the IMF Survey, 25 July 1983). Net use of Fund credit by developing countries increased even further in 1982, to SDR 6.1 billion. According to the same source, net use of Fund credit by developing countries reached SDR6.0 billion in the first half of 1983. (That is a level as high as net borrowing from the IMF during the whole of 1982!) A large part of recent increases in net Fund lending has been geared towards Latin American countries (see Graph 1).

One of the main factors which explained the IMF's increased lending was its greater availability of financial resources. On the one hand, the seventh review of Fund quotas became effective in December 1980, leading to an increase of total Fund quotas from about SDR 40 billion to SDR 60 billion. On the other hand, the IMF borrowed significant sums in the early 1980s: in particular, it entered into a medium-term loan agreement with the Saudi Arabian Monetary Agency, for up to SDR 8 billion and a short-term loan agreement with the central banks and official agencies of certain industrial countries of up to SDR 1.3 billion.

The Fund's future ability to lend will be further enhanced by the recent agreement (in principle) to increase Fund quotas by 47.5 per cent – this is *substantially less than the increase of 100 per cent suggested by developing countries* but higher than the initial US proposal. This agreement will not become effective before the end of 1983 and may in fact be delayed for a longer period. The whole agreement to expand IMF quotas had been put in jeopardy by the difficulties faced in the US Congress to secure approval for the increase in the US quota to the IMF.

Linked to this, problems have arisen in the latter part of 1983 to secure short-term funding for the IMF. As it became more difficult for the IMF to raise a special US$6 billion dollar loan from the industrial countries' central banks and from the Saudi Arabian monetary authorities, the IMF Executive Board temporarily suspended all new loans in September 1983, at the same time there was no increase in its supply of lendable resources. The ability of the IMF to continue large net lending was dramatically curtailed in late 1983.

Given the seriousness of the recent debt crises and the possibility of their recurrence, the industrial countries wished to increase the Fund's usable resources rapidly. To achieve this, the Group of Ten major industrial countries agreed in January 1983 to boost the resources of the General Agreement to Borrow (GAB) system (the financing mechanism used by the Group of Ten to top up the resources of the IMF), and to enlarge access to its funds. They thus agreed to increase GAB resources from SDR 6.4 billion to SDR 17 billion; more importantly, they broadened access to GAB drawings, formerly limited to Group of Ten members, to all IMF members. However, although managed by the IMF authorities, they do not have an automatic right to use these resources, the GAB members who provide the funds have the power to allow or disallow a drawing. It has been reported (*South*, March 1983) that US officials stated clearly that the release of funds from the GAB pool to any Third World country would probably be triggered only by a major financial crisis – one that threatened the industrialised countries' banking systems.

Demand for IMF credit has been growing, as the possibility of obtaining private credits without the Fund's 'seal of approval' has become more limited and as the sums available for borrowing from the IMF have become larger. Under the policy of enlarged access, approved early in 1981, countries may borrow up to 450 per cent of their quotas from the Fund to support high conditionality programmes. This was an important increase relative to the situation during most of the seventies, when a country could purchase usually up to 165 per cent under an extended arrangement and previously up to 100 per cent under a stand-by. The loan made to India in late 1981 (of SDR 5 billion), the largest ever made by the Fund, was the first to show the increased scale of Fund lending. The recent large loans agreed by the Fund for several Latin American borrowers also indicate the much greater scale of IMF lending *in the early eighties*. Access to Fund resources (as proportion of countries' quotas) will be reduced, if and when quotas are increased.

Official Development Assistance flows

The increase in IMF lending to developing countries during the early eighties is in sharp contrast to the evolution of official development assistance flows. According to the 1982 OECD *Development Cooperation Review*, total flows of official development assistance (ODA) from the industrial countries declined (even in nominal terms) in 1981 by more than 6 per cent, falling from US$27.3 billion in 1980 to US$ 25.6 billion in 1981. The OECD publication attributes the fall in 1981 ODA commitments mainly to delays or reductions in contributions to multilateral banks, particularly to the International Development Association (IDA). To this trend is added a decline in ODA from the OPEC countries, which fell from US$8.9 billion in 1980 to US$7.8 billion in 1981. Considering that COMECON net ODA disbursements are reported to be constant, total net disbursements of ODA declined from 1980 to 1981.

At the level of multilateral official flows, however, new measures have been implemented which may have an impact on sustaining private capital flows to developing countries at a time when commercial lenders have become very cautious. These new techniques, introduced for an experimental two-year period by the World Bank in January 1983, would imply a particular boost to the finance of projects in developing countries and thus could potentially be of relevance to mining projects in developing countries.

The new co-financing techniques announced – which are intended to supplement rather than replace the World Bank's present co-financing with the private sector – have been devised with two aims in view: to provide a measure of greater security to commercial lenders participating in the new arrangements, and to improve the terms of commercial lending to developing country borrowers by a lengthening of maturities.

Under the existing system, the World Bank and the commercial banks enter into separate loan agreements with the borrowing country; under the new arrangements, the Bank will participate in the lending from commercial sources in addition to making a direct loan.

Up to US$500 million has been set aside for some 15 to 20 trial projects generating, it is to be hoped, about $2,500 million of total co-financing. The three new techniques to be tested are:

1. Direct financial participation by the World Bank in the later maturities of a commercial loan. Repayments of principal would be made first to the commercial lenders and then, when they had been fully repaid, the payments would be applied to the World Bank's share.

2. Contingent participation by the Bank in the later maturities of a commercial loan which would be initially financed by commercial lenders. The commercial bank loan would be at a variable interest rate but the annual debt-service by the borrower would be fixed. If interest rates rise and amortisation is not completed on the original schedule, the Bank would have a contingent commitment to finance the remainder of the principal.

3. Guarantees of the later maturities of a commercial loan. Under

this option the World Bank would not participate in the commercial loan but would guarantee repayment of the later part.

The changes stem in part from the emphasis placed on co-financing by the World Bank since 1982, although prior to that the Bank had taken part in co-financing projects. Between July 1973 and December 1982 the Bank provided US$31 billion for 784 co-financing projects. Most of these were with official lenders, which provided US$13.5 billion, and export credit guarantee agencies, which provided another US$10.8 billion. There were 96 co-financings with commercial banks, under which those banks provided US$9 billion.

PART THREE: FINAL REMARKS

9 CONCLUSIONS AND SOME POLICY PROPOSALS

Future Prospects

The future prospects for international financing of developing countries are not very encouraging if current economic and financial trends follow those prevalent in the early eighties. If economic recovery in the industrial countries is minimal and delayed as many observers still fear, then the current account deficits of developing countries may continue to rise rapidly, thus leading to heavy demands upon international finance to cover this gap. Thus, estimates produced by Morgan Guaranty (*World Financial Markets*, February 1984) suggest that *even if the 21 major developing country borrowers make a major and sustained 'adjustment' effort* (which assumes Gross Domestic Product (GDP) growth in 1983 lower than the population growth – but implying 5.0 per cent GDP growth in 1983 and 1985) as long as industrial countries' economic growth is very low, the current account deficits of developing countries will continue to grow at a very high pace. Morgan Guaranty estimates that in this pessimistic 'scenario' the current account deficits of the 21 major LDC borrowers alone would increase from an estimated US$64 billion in 1982 to US$102 billion in 1985. Naturally, as a result debt would increase dramatically.

Recent developments in the Euromarkets (see Chapter 8) would indicate that the nature of private banks' lending to developing countries may be changing rather significantly. Particularly if the world recession continues, their net lending to developing countries will probably continue to grow very slowly or even decline, and will continue to be largely of a defensive and involuntary nature. It is to be expected that very large private banks (already heavily involved in lending to LDCs) will try to lend enough to try to avoid economic collapse or default on their major debts. However, banks not already too heavily involved, may continue to attempt to cut their exposure altogether. Nor can it be expected that new banks will join the club of international lenders to developing countries. Thus, one of the main sources of expansion in the past – entrance of new banks into the LDC market – will surely be inoperative in the near future.

Within private bank lending, there will be switches to 'safer' lending, e.g. lending less for balance of payments purposes and more for projects.

Furthermore, banks are increasingly showing preference for lending through the technique of 'project finance', which guarantees them the income for repayment from the initial sales of the project. Simultaneously, private bankers will continue to pursue, as far as possible, the creation of mechanisms which increasingly involve official institutions (e.g. World Bank, regional development banks) in helping to guarantee their debt or grant cross-default clauses. The facility approved within the GAB (see Chapter 8) certainly is a further step in that direction. It is a cause of concern for developing countries in general, and the Latin American countries in particular, that such mechanisms will not so much alleviate their problems as make lending safer for private banks. However, developing countries could benefit indirectly, if increased stability in capital markets led to stimulation of new lending.

The International Monetary Fund is the only major institution which may if its resources are increased, go on expanding its lending significantly. (However, this was put in serious doubt in September 1983, when all new IMF loans were suspended because of constraints on the Fund's usable resources.) The demand for IMF credits is widespread. Expanded lending by the Fund – though welcome in itself – may, however, have very problematic effects on developing countries' growth and development if Fund conditionality remains unchanged. In fact, the debate on IMF conditionality has become much more important in the eighties than it was in the last decade. The Fund has been lending more, and its 'seal of approval' has even greater influence in obtaining credit from other sources; furthermore, a much higher proportion of its loans – than in the past decade – are in the upper credit tranches, which implies more stringent conditionality. The exact nature of the conditionality to be applied by the Fund will, therefore, inevitably continue to be intensely debated, both at the international level (North-South debates, UNCTAD, etc) as well as during specific negotiations between the IMF and deficit countries.

If current trends are projected, the prospects for developing countries are rather dismal. Not only will the low-income countries, whose growth record in the seventies was already very poor, continue to face equally or more serious external constraints on their growth; but also those countries, including several of the large Latin American economies, which in the seventies achieved high rates of growth, will probably see their situation worsen. If the world economic environment continues to be unfavourable, and if private financial flows are increasingly difficult to obtain, the options open even for the more industrialised developing countries may become severely restricted. The pressure, particularly from the lenders, will be for those countries to 'adjust', which in a depressed or slow growing world environment may mean in the medium term to grow less!

The developments outlined above imply that the crisis in the industrial countries' banking system might be resolved – or at least postponed – but that the crisis in growth and development of the Third World will continue or perhaps even accelerate.

However, a very unfavourable international environment may tempt debtor countries – particularly those whose governments are very radical and/or are faced with a very critical situation – to declare a moratorium on their debt, or even declare an open default. The need to avoid such a situation – particularly damaging for industrial countries' banks and economies, but also potentially harmful for the developing countries themselves – may provoke the governments of industrial countries into more positive action.

At a national level, within developing countries, the effects of international difficulties – in trade and finance – may have one positive effect. It may influence developing countries to orient their development in a manner less reliant upon the international economy – to put greater emphasis on internal savings rather than on foreign borrowing, to place greater importance on production for the internal or regional market rather than for the international one. The trends may be positive in the medium term, but will be insufficient in the short term to solve the serious crisis in growth and development facing developing countries in general, and Latin America in particular.

Some Policy Proposals

There is, however, a more optimistic alternative for the future; its basic requirements are a sustained and strong economic recovery in the industrial countries and higher net financial inflows, at more appropriate terms, to Latin America. We shall discuss these in some detail here.

Sustained Growth in the Industrial Countries

Naturally, a sustained and buoyant economic recovery by the industrial countries, particularly if accompanied by lower interest rates, would be a major boost for Latin American countries' growth prospects; given a certain level of external financial net flows, higher growth in industrial countries would allow higher growth in Latin American countries.

Regression analysis relating growth among developing countries to growth among industrial countries for 1960-77 showed that for every percentage point decline in the growth of industrial countries, that of developing countries declined by 0.23 per cent.[1]

Some analysts have in fact argued that the simultaneous world recession in different industrial countries is the principal source of the current setbacks to world development; consequently, a major contribution to growth and development in the Third World could be effected if industrial countries accelerated their own growth. This would seem to be somewhat easier at a time of relatively low inflation in most industrial countries, and at a time when most current account surpluses are in fact concentrated in industrial countries' economies (such as Japan, United Kingdom, Switzerland, Netherlands, West Germany and Canada).[2]

It seems that if industrial countries are ever to return to the growth rates of the 1960s, they will need to revive demand management. Given the degree of interdependence that now exists, demand management will almost inevitably require policy co-ordination at least as great as that resulting from OECD surveillance within the context of the Bretton-Woods system in the 1960s. Co-ordinated expansion does not necessarily mean that every country expands at the same time or pace, but rather that expansion is planned and co-ordinated among the major industrial countries to avoid either the situation where a country which tries to lead expansion alone is penalised, or the problems of simultaneous recessionary measures being taken in several countries.

It is noteworthy that it is not only 'Keynesians' who ascribe a significant part of the blame for the 1980-3 recession to failures of policy co-ordination. Arguing from a 'global monetarist' perspective, Ronald McKinnon (1982) has pointed to the sharp deceleration in the rate of aggregate monetary growth of the major covertible-currency countries as the principal source of the recent industrial countries' recession. He argues that this deceleration was clearly unintended and resulted accidentally as a by-product of asymmetrical sterilisation policies between the US and other countries.

Co-ordination of macro-economic policies may be pursued either by laying down a set of rules intended to ensure consistency if pursued by all parties, or by periodic discussions to promote the adoption of mutually consistent policies. The main advocate of a rule-based approach has in recent years been McKinnon; most advocates of co-ordination, have, however, envisaged periodic international discussions to co-ordinate either the objectives or the commitments of economic policy. Proposals to agree to a consistent set of current account targets were much discussed in the OECD in the 1960s; these discussions were somewhat academic, however, as countries did not actually wield any effective policy weapons to influence the current account outcome if it appeared likely to differ from the target. Several writers (e.g. Solomon, 1975) reopened the subject after the first oil price rise, stressing that attempts to pass on the oil deficits could lead to competitive devaluations, payments restrictions, or deflation. Nothing was done; it has been said (Williamson, 1983b) that with the benefit of hindsight provided by the debt crisis, such agreed current account targets might have provided a valuable early warning sign in that the large industrial countries passed on the entire oil deficit. Similarly, if there was some collective guidance as to how much borrowing might be appropriate in the future – the IMF (or another central world organisation) could develop a set of current account targets – this would provide some reassurance that attempts by deficit countries to adjust would not be thwarted by the reactions of surplus countries, nor lead to a downward spiral in world income.

The wish to stabilise world income around a full capacity trend has brought about proposals to co-ordinate fiscal and monetary instruments for this purpose. This has been, for example, very clearly articulated by a statement of 26 economists at a Conference at the Institute for International Economists held in Washington in 1982 – *Promoting World Recovery: a Statement by 26 Economists from 14 Countries*, which outlined a model for co-ordinated measures to support concerted global recovery.

Although the existence of a more appropriate co-ordination forum and mechanisms might be helpful in achieving such targets and might possibly improve the chances for such – or other proposals – being implemented, the main obstacles are the political and economic strategies employed by most major industrial countries; most of these countries still seem to continue to attach greater priority to the control of inflation, of public expenditure and money supply than to achieving economic growth. One reason for this is that they do not acknowledge fully the interdependence between their own economies and those of the rest of the world, and, therefore, they mainly take into account the national and not the international consequences of such actions. Thus, the main hope for a co-ordinated expansion in industrial countries seems to lie in the short term in the governments of industrial countries adopting a different approach and favouring such a policy.

Once such a change of attitude has occurred, further long-term institutional changes could be discussed and implemented, which would provide an appropriate framework for policy co-ordination. Such an institution, if created, might incorporate some of the elements discussed above in Keynes's Plan for a Clearing Union, with the purpose of exerting automatic pressure on surplus countries to encourage them to reflate; it could incorporate also more recent proposals, such as gradually transforming a reformed IMF into a world central bank (for example, see Cooper, 1983). The advantage of discussing co-ordinated macro-economic expansion in the major industrial countries within the forum of a reformed IMF would be that it would guarantee multilateral participation in such discussions, for although the main issues relate to the policies of a few major economies, their impact goes beyond the borders of those countries. For example, the governments of developing countries would in such discussions stress the need for economic recovery in industrial countries to be accompanied by lower interest rates, as the latter has a major effect on their own economies. The credibility, legitimacy and stability of the global economic order depends, as the 1983 Commonwealth Secretariat Report points out, on universal participation in the major international decision-making forums; naturally such multilateralised consultations do not preclude the process of co-ordination by narrower groups of countries, for example, the Group of Ten. Some of the functions which a *reformed* IMF would have in the context of regulating national economies so as to achieve sustained and non-inflationary growth, for example, providing compensatory finance and/or issue SDRs in a counter-cyclical way, would be linked to the issues of creating appropriate levels of international liquidity and adequate net financial flows to developing countries, and, as such, will be discussed in the next section.

Finally, in this context it is essential to stress that reduction of developing countries' debt problems (and avoidance of a major debt crisis) would help to overcome a major obstacle for rapid economic recovery in both industrialised and developing countries.

Liquidity and Finance for Developing Countries, with Particular Reference to Latin America

The proposals for enhancing liquidity available to developing countries, to enable them to sustain their growth and development tend to be made increasingly at two *separate, though complementary, levels.*[3] On the one hand, are proposals for immediate, short-term and often urgent action to help overcome the current problems and foreign exchange crises facing them. On the other hand, are proposals for a major review of the world monetary system, leading to a major reform in this system, to make it more appropriate to the current needs of industrialised and developing countries than at present is the case. Many analysts are somewhat inhibited in pressing for such major reforms in the system, given that governments/parliaments of the major industrial countries are very reluctant to contemplate even relatively minor changes (e.g. making a moderate rise in the size of the International Monetary Fund's quotas), or are reducing previously accepted levels of official flows (e.g. problems of sustaining IDA funding).

However, the limitations of the existing international monetary system, as well as its negative impact on the growth prospects of developing countries – and, therefore, the world – are becoming increasingly evident. The need for a major reform of the system, therefore, becomes more urgent, even though the short term political feasibility is limited. In this context, pressing for such a major review (or a 'new Bretton-Woods') can be seen as an effective *complement* (*and not as a substitute*) to taking immediate steps. In this respect, the proposals discussed below are on the whole mutually consistent but operationally relatively independent. Such initiatives *could be pursued individually* when support for them develops; if support for making sweeping changes to existing arrangements increased significantly, then these proposals and others could be simultaneously adopted, at what might be dubbed a 'new Bretton-Woods'.

Before examining these proposals in some detail it seems important to stress that developing countries, grouped together for example in the Group of 24 on International Monetary Affairs and in the Group of 77 (as well as other regional groupings) have consistently supported major reforms in the international monetary system (see, for example, 'Outline for a Programme of Action on International Monetary Reform', *IMF Survey*, 15 October 1979 and 'Communique of the Group of 24', *IMF Survey*, 21 February 1983). In fact it has been argued (Helleiner, 1983) that the developing countries are emerging as the main defenders of the original Bretton-Woods principles and their implementation within the existing context.

Amongst possible measures to make more adequate provisions for developing countries' finance and international liquidity, the following are worth discussing:

1. measures to sustain, particularly in the short and medium term, private credit flows, and to attempt to create mechanisms to make pri-

vate financial flows more appropriate to the needs of developing countries

2. measures to sustain or increase the role of multilateral official institutions

3. increased South-South co-operation, possibly through the creation of new institutions

4. restructuring existing debt

To provide continuity with the previous analysis, it should be pointed out that some of the proposals to be discussed under (2) and (3) and to a smaller extent (1), will be linked to the search for a new dynamic participator willing and able to generate flows of external finance for the developing countries in general, and for Latin America in particular. Measures will also be examined to sustain or even increase *net* flows from participators who had played a dynamic role in the past, but are unwilling to continue doing so for the present.

Measures such as these are particularly important to avoid net flows (defined as disbursements minus principal repayments) becoming low or even negative, and – even more difficult – to avoid net transfers (defined as net flows minus interest and profit remittances) becoming strongly negative. As mentioned in Chapter 2, in Latin America during 1982 net transfers reached a very high negative amount (of approximately – US$15 billion), with serious consequences for the growth and development of nearly all the Latin American countries.

1. Measures to sustain, particularly in the short and medium term, private credit flows and to create mechanisms to make private financial flows more appropriate to the needs of developing countries.

Many proposals have already been made in this area, although very limited action has as yet been taken; it is important to note that particularly since late 1982, as financial distress has spread, bankers themselves have increasingly made proposals in this area. Several of the proposals attempt to combine measures which will make the perceived risks of such flows smaller for the private lenders (e.g. via some guarantee mechanism) with measures to make the mechanisms through which such flows are granted more appropriate for developing countries' needs (e.g. through more favourable financial terms implying longer maturities and lower fixed interest rates).

One of the first of such proposals was one put forward by the Mexican government at the meeting of the Development Committee, held in Mexico City in April 1978. It proposed to establish a fund which would be financed by the issue of 15-year bonds on the international capital markets; these bonds would be guaranteed by the governments of developed (and perhaps some developing) countries. The funds would be used to grant long-term loans (with maturity of 15 years or so), to be used only for the purchase of capital goods from other developing countries or from developed countries whose governments had contributed to the bond issue.

A more recent proposal, given high priority by the UNCTAD Secretariat (1983) and strongly supported by the Group of 77 was to establish an International Export Credit Guarantee Facility. This facility would guarantee export credits of developing countries, mainly for capital goods, so as to improve the marketability of export credit papers. This facility would not engage in direct lending, but by providing a strong guarantee (backed by multilateral financial institutions such as the World Bank and industrialised countries, and counter-guaranteed by national agencies in the exporting developing countries) would help developing countries rediscount their paper on favourable terms in international capital markets.

More recently, there have been several broad proposals to help *sustain all types of private flows to developing countries*, allow access to those perceived as less 'creditworthy' by the markets and *provide longer-term, fixed interest finance to developing countries.*

Thus, the Chairman of a large British merchant bank, Mackworth-Young (1983), has proposed that *all* new international borrowing – and possibly also debts already contracted – by developing countries from commercial banks should take the form of bonds, guaranteed by some supranational agency, backed up by the world's main central banks. John Williamson (1983b) has also suggested long-term *indexed* bonds be issued by an agency such as the IMF or the World Bank acting as the agent for a collective of developing countries, with partial guarantees provided by the stock of IMF gold or other assets. One interesting aspect of his proposal is that it attempts to define more precisely the source for such long-term funding, including tapping the portfolios of pension funds and insurance companies in industrial countries, institutions that have long-dated liabilities and that are more interested in real yields than in being assured of a given nominal book value at each moment of time. (Williamson points out that in the past low-absorbing OPEC governments would have been natural sources for such bonds; indeed his initial proposal was largely geared towards them.)

Official institutions, such as the World Bank and some of the regional development banks, have also been discussing expanded use of guarantees to provide political risk insurance. An American private banker, Frank (1983) has recently suggested that public and private political risk insurance programmes might be combined (where public insurance would cover the longer maturities). Some private insurance companies have recently developed new political risk insurance programmes to support loan and equity investments in developing countries. One example is a programme developed to finance short- and medium-term export receivables; the notes based on those receivables have received high ratings in US private and public securities markets.

Finally, there are even broader proposals aiming at averting the damaging effects of a major financial crisis on private lending to developing countries, and particularly to help sustain private lending in times of widespread fear of defaults and financial crisis, accompanied by an increasing amount of reschedulings and arrears. Recently Lipton and Griffith-Jones (1983) have suggested the need for an *explicit International Lender of Last Resort (ILLR)*, backed by the central banks of the industrialised countries, and accompanied by far stricter supervision of commercial banks by those central banks. Such a combination should stabilise the growth of private lending in 'euphoria' stages and minimise its contraction during critical times. This particular proposal would accept – in the case of banks running into serious difficulties because of non-payment of sovereign debt at a large discount – the bad debts which the banks have in their portfolio as 'collateral' for using the International Lender of Last Resort Facility. Thus, the banks would pay a contribution towards this operation, but would be saved from bankruptcy. Afterwards the International Lender of Last Resort could negotiate the repayment of debts with developing countries' borrowers – at lengthened maturities and lower interest rates – considering that it had bought these debts at a discount. The lower 'debt burden' on developing countries would remove an important constraint on their (as well as the world's) growth. Even if the International Lender of Last Resort Facility was never actually used, its existence would encourage private bankers to sustain and possibly increase present as well as future credit flows to developing countries; this would be its important function.

In evaluating the potential impact if such proposals were implemented, the crucial issue is to determine whether such mechanisms would *de facto* imply *additionality to existing net flows.*

It has often been argued that funds allocated to provide any guarantee facility – whether subscribed by industrial countries' central banks directly or via institutions such as the World Bank or the IMF – could be alternatively used for lending directly to developing countries by governments or international public institutions. However, a guarantee facility offers a higher gearing ratio than the World Bank or the Regional Development Banks, with the result that the finance diverted to such a guarantee fund would increase total net lending.

The additional financial flows resulting from such a facility would be particularly important in times, such as the current one, when there is relatively widespread financial distress and fears that such distress might be transformed into a major financial crisis. Proposals guaranteeing all commercial lending to developing countries by an explicit International Lender of Last Resort Facility would be crucial for the maintenance of confidence, and for sustaining private flows to developing countries in critical times. It might have the further advantage that it could be combined with the *introduction of more appropriate financial terms (such as longer maturities and lower fixed interest rates)* for lending to the Third World, stronger supervision by central banks of commercial bank lending and better distribution *amongst developing countries*. Although highly desirable, the establishment of some sort of supranational lender of last resort may, perhaps, be some way off. It is seen by some observers as taking sovereignty from participating central banks, while raising difficult questions of how banks from non-participating countries should be treated – particularly those off-shore centres which have no national lender of last resort capacity. A serious problem is the potentially high cost of such a facility, to which central banks of industrial countries are currently unwilling *a priori* to commit themselves, preferring a case-by-case approach, in which they think they have greater control. As the debt crises become increasingly greater and more widespread, the potential cost of *not* setting up such a facility – with the risk of major collapses in even the largest private banks – will increasingly seem to outweigh the cost of the facility, even for the industrial countries.

2. Measures to sustain or increase the role of multilateral official institutions.

In the medium term, it seems clearly essential to increase and reform the role of existing multilateral official institutions. Naturally such an emphasis would also be desirable in the short term, but it seems less feasible politically. Given the recent problems for IMF and IDA funding in particular, it would seem that, in most, though not all aspects relating to multilateral official institutions, the current debates are whether to maintain existing flows in real terms or to curtail them!

Perhaps the most crucial changes in the medium term should be carried out in the role of the International Monetary Fund, not merely so that its lending is expanded but so that it is transformed into an institution similar to a world central bank. It would seem that in their pursuit of such major reforms, developing countries need to attempt simultaneously a double and difficult task: *encouraging the IMF to move towards a more key, global role whilst ensuring that during this process the IMF represents increasingly the genuine interests and needs of different types of developing countries.*

In the short term, there seems to be a proven case, convincingly argued by the UNCTAD Secretariat, the Group of 24 and the Group of 77, amongst others, for an urgent and sizeable allocation of special drawing rights (SDRs).

It is argued that the new issue of SDRs must be large, to compensate for *the decline in total international liquidity* occurring in the early eighties, and to help finance deficits if world economic recovery is to be sustained. An SDR allocation has important advantages in the current context. It would help restore the ratio of SDR to non gold reserves to previous levels, as this ratio has been deteriorating; more importantly SDR allocations *do not create repayment obligations*, which is particularly crucial at a time when countries' debt-service ratios are already so high that many countries are unable to service their debts without major deflation of their economies. Finally, there is a problem of timing; measures to enlarge lending by means of existing official institutions, or by creating new ones will take time to implement whereas there is an urgent need for expanding liquidity, particularly for the developing countries. Several of the proposals for a new issue of SDRs argue convincingly the case for a higher proportion of this issue than in the past to be allocated to developing countries. However, such proposals will undoubtedly be resisted by the largest industrial countries and may delay the approval of any issue of SDRs at all.

More broadly, the objective of a single currency reserve system (on similar principles even though involving different practical arrangements to those proposed by Keynes and Triffin, as well as others) based on the SDR remains clearly a desirable one for the longer term. Considering the increasing problems and inequities caused by the present multi-currency system, it seems important to aim for such a single-currency system controlled by a supranational authority. Concrete measures may be taken to initiate such a transition – in particular, those which would make use of the SDR more attractive, by overcoming the limited facilities available for making direct payments in SDRs. Examples of such measures are: authorisation and stimulus for private holding of SDRs, the creation of SDR clearing arrangements that would permit SDR transactions between private banks and the official sector and the fostering of an inter-bank private market in SDRs. Greater use of SDRs by multilateral development banks would also be important.

Of even greater significance (as discussed in Polak, 1979) for the establishment of an IMF-based liquidity system would be the merger of the IMF's general account – which relates to its normal operations – with its special drawings account. Such a consolidation would not only greatly simplify IMF lending, but would also avoid the need for national currencies in IMF operations, and open the way for its playing a role more akin to that of a global central bank, with the capacity to create additional liquidity as required (possibly combined at a later stage, with the ability to influence the issue of liquidity created by the national authorities or by the commercial banks).

An important feature of such an extension of the SDR is that the IMF could more easily issue them in a counter-cyclical way, providing for more in periods of slump and providing fewer or none in periods of world economic boom. If commercial deposits were developed in SDRs, such variations in SDR issues might influence economic activity not only by their impact on government policies, but also by making the commercial banking system more or less liquid in terms of SDRs, and so influencing private bank lending. To allow for this counter-cyclical function for the SDR, the procedures for SDR allocations should be simplified to allow for year-to-year variations and permit quick decisions, instead of the prolonged process of consultations that now occurs for allocations that are to cover a period of five years. The technical difficulties (even though important) are clearly of less significance than the difficulty in achieving political support of the major industrial countries for such changes.

Another significant improvement in IMF provision of liquidity to developing countries (in this case of a low-conditionality type) would be by means of an enlarged and amended Compensatory Financing Facility (CFF).

In fact, the first change in the rules of the international monetary system that the developing countries succeeded in securing was the introduction of the IMF Compensatory Financing Facility in 1963. Latin American governments and ECLA (CEPAL) played a major role in establishing the technical need for such a facility. This facility has since become accepted as a necessary mechanism to mitigate the adverse impact of fluctuations in export earnings of developing countries on their development process, by attempting to maintain unaffected import capacity despite fluctuations in export earnings caused by external events. The CFF provides for low-conditionality drawings from the IMF to finance temporary shortfalls in export earnings below the estimated trend, subject to limits set by the size of a country's quota and the size of the estimated shortfall.

The CFF became in the seventies a major facility for providing payments assistance by the Fund to member countries, especially developing ones. However, there is clear evidence that borrowing under the facility remained modest in comparison with deterioration in the terms of trade experienced by developing countries, particularly during the last recession. The main problems of the existing *modus operandi* of the CFF are: the quota limits on maximum drawings (this is clearly the most important constraint), the calculation of export shortfalls in nominal terms and a formula for repayments which is not linked to the recovery of export earnings (see, Griffith-Jones, 1982).

The Group of 24, as well as the UNCTAD Secretariat, has proposed a liberalisation of the CFF in order to provide full coverage of shortfalls, preferably by making it independent of quota limits. There is also widespread support for the shortfall formula to be reviewed and expressed in real terms (so as to take account of real import capacity rather than nominal), and for making repayments more closely linked to a country's recovery of export earnings. Furthermore, there is much support for such proposals in academic circles, which emphasise particularly the important counter-cyclical impact that an expanded CFF could have – both on developing countries and the world economy – thus helping to break the vicious circles of recession and financial distress characterising the recent period. In this respect, proposals for an enlarged CFF may coincide with a greater use of SDR allocations, which could be used to finance such an enlarged CFF. As the largest aggregate shortfalls in export earnings are likely to take place under recessionary conditions, such SDR issues would be least likely to be inflationary, but would be helpful in sustaining recovery in the countries most seriously affected by foreign exchange constraints.

Proposals such as increasing unconditional international liquidity via SDRs and/or low-conditionality liquidity via the Compensatory Financing Facility imply that in the future help in financing developing countries' deficits would be found in supranational agencies, engaged not in pursuing their own perceived interests but the perceived best interests of the world economy. Although such mechanisms are consistent with the increasing internationalisation and interdependence of the world economy, it is unfortunately not clear whether it will be politically feasible, particularly in the current climate under which many government seem to – temporarily at least – withdraw even from existing multilateral commitments.

Current trends have at the moment, however, resulted in the IMF playing an increased role in the financing of developing countries' deficits, through different mechanisms to those proposed above, that is via its *high-conditionality lending facilities* (such as stand-by and extended fund facility arrangements). This seems a desirable development in the sense of implying a larger role for the multilateral official global agency, which may with time form the basis for a world central bank, although it would seem preferable to have a greater proportion of unconditional or low-conditional liquidity provided by the Fund. Furthermore, to assure that expanded high-conditionality lending serves effectively the needs and interests of deficit countries which borrow from the Fund (and particularly the developing countries who are its major 'clients'), it seems essential to assure *a major reform of the conditionality under which the IMF lends*. It is for this reason that the much debated issue of IMF conditionality becomes increasingly crucial if the IMF's role, in extending its own lending and having a catalystic effect on other flows, increases.

In fact, both the IMF and the World Bank impose certain conditions before agreeing to substantial loans – the IMF for its upper tranche lending, the World Bank for its structural adjustment loans. Both types of conditionality have been subject to criticism, and proposals have been made for reform. Since the World Bank's structural adjustment loans form only a small part of its total lending and since the Bank generally requires that the Fund conditions also be met, it is sensible to focus on Fund conditionality.

It is generally agreed that some conditionality for countries in acute balance of payments difficulties is required in order to secure improvement in the external payments position. However, Fund conditionality has been criticised in respect of several crucial elements, which include the following critiques: first, for designing its conditions at the level of the individual country, thus failing to take into account the aggregate implication of its required programmes when carried out in a number of countries; secondly, in the objectives implicit in its programmes; thirdly, in the instruments it considers and, fourthly, in relation to the 'performance' variables adopted. (See, for example, Dell, 1981, and Stewart and Sengupta, 1982, as well as a brief discussion in Chapter 6.)

Proposals for reform involve changes in the nature of Fund conditionality in order to meet these criticisms. Apart from the content of the programmes, it has been proposed that the method of negotiation should be changed. Instead of the Fund presenting governments with a programme, the programmes should be devised with active participation of the country concerned, other interested parties and independent observers. Programmes arrived at in this way would be more acceptable to the country and therefore more likely to be adhered to. They would take into account a country's own priorities and its preferences as to instruments.

A major thrust of proposals for reform is that conditionality should be concerned with structural aspects as well as demand. Supply is now included formally in Fund programmes, but in practice this has not made a major difference since the main emphasis has continued to be on control of demand, while supply conditions have been interpreted as largely a matter of price incentives, and not a question of building up investment in potential export and import substituting industries. For many countries the main cause of balance of payments problems is *not* excessive domestic expenditure, but changes in the nature of the world economy (including deteriorating terms of trade) for which *an appropriate response is to improve their productive structure, rather than reduce demand.*

Alternative policies for adjustment would vary from country to country, according to the specific history, problems, preferences and opportunities of each. Consequently, no single alternative conditionality is proposed. But a major emphasis should be on policy changes to produce supply increases that will secure improvement in the balance of payments in the medium term.

Emphasis on structural changes to secure improvements in the balance of payments involves a longer-term perspective than emphasis on demand reduction; as a result, this would imply that Fund finance should be medium term, rather than short term, and should be greater in amount.

A major criticism of the Fund operations lies in its failure to 'aggregate' as described above. As a response to this, it has been proposed that the Fund should take into account the state of the world economy and the aggregate implications of its programmes in devising particular country programmes (see, Cooper, 1983). Similarly, it has been repeatedly proposed that the Fund should also address its programmes to *surplus* countries. Following similar principles to those advocated by Keynes, the Committee of 20 for International Monetary Reform, which met in the early seventies, recommended the need for 'effective and symmetrical adjustment procedures', and that graduated pressure be applied to any country in persistent imbalance, whether surplus or deficit.

In relation to performance targets of fund programmes (which are so often missed), these could be specified with agreed margins of deviation and linked in a pre-agreed form with key exogenous variables such as the prices of exports and imports, international interest rates, etc. These might even be more appropriately replaced by broader assessments of economic policy and performance. New performance targets (e.g. linked with sustained income and/or consumption of poor people, within countries) could be explored.

Multilateral Development Banks

In this chapter, a great deal of space has been given to the IMF because it is the principal international institution capable of acting swiftly in the present difficult situation. However, multilateral development banks, including their soft loan funds, are an extremely important and distinct source of *long-term finance for developing countries*, and they account for a high proportion of total net disbursements to developing countries from all sources. Furthermore, they have increasingly (through co-financing and other mechanisms) acted as a catalyst for other sources, particularly private lending. Considering the large demand for long-term financial flows to developing countries and the limited willingness or capacity – under current circumstances – of commercial banks, bond markets or foreign investors to supply them, there is a strong argument for expanding the role of multilateral development banks.

To sustain increased lending, it has been suggested that the subscribed capital base of the World Bank be enlarged (without necessarily requiring any or at least not a large increase in paid-in capital) and/or that the 'gearing ratio' be increased. The political feasibility of large increases in subscribed capital, even though desirable in the short term, are put in doubt by recent developments, in particular by the serious difficulties to obtain approval from the US Congress for the replenishment of the World Bank's soft loan aim, IDA; the proposal for an increased gearing ratio could thus perhaps become more feasible in the current political climate.

Furthermore, in current circumstances, it might be useful for the

World Bank to expand the new co-financing measures it adopted in early 1983 (described in Chapter 8). Similarly, it would be valuable if such (or other) co-financing measures were rapidly introduced on an experimental basis in other multilateral development banks, such as the regional and sub-regional development banks.

More generally, the role of regional development banks also needs to be expanded, particularly in relation to the provision of funds for regional activities, such as the financing of regional and sub-regional payments arrangements – so as to cease the foreign exchange constraints on the maintenance and expansion of inter-regional trade – the creation of regional projects and the refinancing or guaranteeing of credits to finance exports to other countries, regionally or otherwise.

3. Increased South-South co-operation, possibly through the creation of new institutions.

Particularly since the late seventies, there have been increased calls for greater South-South co-operation (or inter-regional co-operation among developing countries) both in trade and finance.

When OPEC surpluses were very large, the possibility of creating large new 'Southern' financial institutions was strongly debated. These would provide or direct flow of finance from surplus developing countries (in particular the major oil exporters) to deficit countries without relying on the intermediation of 'Northern' institutions. The most prominent of these proposals was that presented by Algeria and Venezuela in December 1978 for a Third World Development Agency based on a development of the OPEC Fund for International Development. Recently, another proposal, calling for the establishment of a South Bank (presented at UNCTAD Vl), incorporated many of the functions of the earlier proposals for a South-South financial institution.

The South Bank would not rely for its funding – as previous schemes had proposed – exclusively on the surpluses of major oil exporters (which have in any case significantly declined since 1982). More broadly, it would base its funding on developing countries with strong reserve position and high *per capita* income (such as Saudi Arabia) as well as countries with significantly lower income, but with a relatively comfortable balance of payments and reserves position (e.g. Colombia). The proposal assumes a direct contribution by developing countries in convertible foreign exchange of a small fraction of their total reserves (estimated at 1.5 per cent of their 1982 foreign exchange reserves).

The feasibility of a South Bank (or other such major South institution) is put into question by the fact that even when several developing countries had major current account surpluses, their governments were unable to agree on creating such an institution. Circumstances may be more difficult now for its establishment – with practically all developing countries having current account deficits, even though several still have large foreign exchange reserves – even though both the need and the technical viability for such an institution is clearly increasing. In a scheme such as this where the new source of finance comes from within the Third World itself, the appeal for such a proposal is greatly increased. If such a scheme, unfortunately, were not to be implemented, greater emphasis on developing country co-operation at a regional level would be desirable.

4. Restructuring existing debt

One of the crucial issues influencing the size and finance of present and future current account deficits of developing countries is the impact of the already accumulated 'debt overhang'.

The impact of past debt on current deficits is clearly illustrated by figures published by the Bank for International Settlements in its 1983 *Annual Report*. With great difficulty and high internal costs, non-OPEC developing countries were able to reduce the non-interest content of their current acount deficit from \$38 billion in 1980 to \$15.5 billion in 1982. However, of this \$22.5 adjustment, \$19.5 billion was offset by a further increase in their net interest payments. This trend is far more spectacular in relation to the three largest borrowers, all Latin American countries – Brazil, Mexico and Argentina – which accounted for 52 per cent of total debt owed by non OPEC LDCs to private banks. Between 1980 and 1982 these three countries' combined current account external deficits remained virtually unchanged at around \$24 billion, *excluding net interest payments (which had increased by approximately \$13.5 billion during those* two years!); the balance of their current account transactions, however, shifted from a \$12 billion deficit to a \$1.5 billion surplus.

There is a wide range of proposals to deal with the problems of debt overhang and debt rescheduling, ranging from procedural proposals to improve the process of debt renegotiation to much more radical suggestions of debt consolidation or rediscounting.

The UNCTAD Secretariat (1983) has, for example, raised the possibility of generalised debt measures; it suggests as an alternative the postponement, on an exceptional basis, of debt payments falling due on official and officially guaranteed loans from developed countries. The implication being for ODA loans that the amortisation payments scheduled during a two-year period could be added at the end of the scheduled repayment period so that all original maturities would be extended by two years. Proposals are also made by UNCTAD to consolidate a large proportion of official and officially guaranteed export credits. Although such proposals would doubtlessly be beneficial – particularly for poorer countries, which rely much more heavily than other developing countries on official debt – it seems unlikely that generalised proposals for debt rescheduling will be acceptable to the industrial countries' governments, the main creditors.

It is interesting that in the case of private debt, several bankers have themselves suggested the possibility of rediscounting and/or consolidating debts of developing countries with private banks. Bankers such as Felix Rohatyn (1983), Bill Mackworth-Young (1983) and others have presented somewhat similar proposals which would lengthen the maturity of and reduce the rate of interest on developing country bank debts. Such proposals are based on the recognition that large volumes of relatively short-term floating-rate debt are very inappropriate for the funding of developing countries' needs, and that unless already existing debts are transformed into more appropriate instruments, debt crises will become a more or less permanent feature in the international economy.

One such proposal suggests that an existing international agency (or a new one) would purchase developing countries' obligations to banks, but at a discount. The developing countries' debts would be renegotiated, and as they had been taken over at a discount, their maturities could be stretched out and interest rates reduced without budgetary cost to the industrial countries. (There are important similarities here with the International Lender of Last Resort proposal previously discussed.) Developing countries would, therefore, have their debt burden somewhat alleviated, and thus be less constrained regarding their growth and development programmes. The banks would pay a cost, but would have the advantage of an alternative mid-way option to keeping loans on their books, or writing them off completely (which are the main options open at present).

It has been said, however, in banking circles that such a scheme *would only be acceptable to banks if matters became much worse, that is if continued rescheduling were no longer possible by existing methods or, presumably, if the risk of default was increased even further.* Fears have also been expressed that the taking of such action might give market signals which are harmful to developing countries' future borrowing prospects. Perhaps most fundamentally, industrial countries and central banks are at present unwilling to back (and/or finance) a supranational agency which would take over such debts. More modest alternatives – such as a proposal for central banks or governments to assist interested banks to convert some short-term developing country debts into longer-term assets, leaving the process of renegotiating or rescheduling medium- and long-term debt unaltered – may be more easily implemented, though having less beneficial impact on developing countries.

In fact, in mid-1983 the foreign exchange situation, particularly in Latin American countries, continues to be serious. Furthermore, Latin American countries are increasingly grouping themselves to discuss jointly their common problems. An important initiative in this respect was the OAS Conference held by Latin American and Caribbean representatives in Caracas at the end of August 1983 to discuss their foreign debt. From such conferences, may emerge effective joint pressures from debtor countries on lenders, both to reschedule existing debt under conditions more favourable for those countries than are currently being agreed, and to press for new flows at more favourable terms to those and other developing countries, either through existing mechanisms and/or new ones. The fear of debt crisis and default can – as at present – lead to a dramatic decline in net lending to developing countries. If correctly used in negotiations (without excessive ideological radicalism), such fear could transform the private bankers into unwilling – but effective – allies towards genuine major changes in the international monetary system that will favour developing countries. Private bankers in the mid-forties opposed attempts at creating very large official multilateral institutions (see, for example Block, 1977), and thus were a major influence in curtailing the size and functions of the IMF and the World Bank. The size of developing countries' debts to banks might suggest that now the banks would be willing to support a major expansion of official multilateral institutions in the eighties. After all, the phrase of Keynes which both bankers and developing country borrowers remember best at present is: 'If you owe one thousand pounds to a bank, you have to worry; if you owe the bank one million pounds, it is the bank which has to worry.'

The debates on the future international monetary system and flows – though requiring a great deal of technical expertise on the part of developing countries – will also require a great deal of political ability in their attempt to transform their weak economic situation into a source of bargaining strength. Industrial countries' private bankers may provide developing countries with unusual support, to the extent that their interests and those of Third World countries coincide. As a result, a new participator for the financing of developing countries may, however unwillingly, emerge on the scene.

Whatever the outcome of current or future negotiations on the international monetary system, the instability and unreliability of net external financial flows to the Third World, particularly in the early eighties, would seem to recommend that developing countries should be wary of development strategies that rely to such an extent as in the seventies on foreign financial flows, and increasingly emphasise greater reliance on national savings to finance their investment programmes.

Notes

1. W. Cline *et al. World Inflation and the Developing Countries* (Brookings, Washington DC, 1981). Other estimates show even a higher impact on developing countries' growth.
2. BIS *Fifty-Third Annual Report* (Basle, June 1983).
3. See, for example, ICIDI (1980) and (1983), as well as UNCTAD Secretariat (1983), Commonwealth Secretariat (1983) and the Group of 77 Declaration made in April 1983 in Buenos Aires.

SELECT BIBLIOGRAPHY

Adler, J. and Kuznets, P. (eds.) *Capital Movements and Economic Developments* International Economic Association, 1967)

Aronson, J.D. *Money and Power* (Sage Publications, Beverley Hills and London, 1977)

Balassa, B. 'Structural Adjustment Policies in Developing Economies', *World Bank Staff Working Paper*, no. 348 (July 1977)

Bank for International Settlements *Annual Report* (Basle, 1977)

Bank for International Settlements, *Annual Report* (Basle, 1981a)

Bank for International Settlements *The Maturity Distribution of International Bank Lending* (Basle, July 1981b)

Bank for International Settlements, several issues, *International Banking Developments* (Basle)

The Banker, several issues (1977)

Billerback K. and Yasugi, Y. 'Private Direct Investment in Developing Countries', *World Bank Staff Working Paper*, no. 348 (July 1977)

Brett, E.A. *The International Monetary Fund, the International Monetary System and the Periphery* (IFDA Dossier, Geneva, Switzerland, March 1979)

Block, F.L. *The Origins of International Monetary Disorder* (University of California Press, 1977)

Buira, A. 'Recession, Inflation and the International Monetary System', *World Development*, vol. 9, nos. 11-12 (1981)

CEPAL News (Santiago de Chile, January 1983)

Chenery, H. and Strout, A. 'Foreign Assistance and Economic Development', *American Economic Review 56* (September 1966), pp. 679-733

Commonwealth Secretariat *Towards a New Bretton-Woods* (Marlborough House, London, August 1983)

Cooper, R. 'The Evolution of the International Monetary Fund towards a World Central Bank', *Study on International Financial and Trading System*, background paper, Commonwealth Secretariat, 1983

Crockett, A. *International Money* (Thomas Nelson and Sons, 1977)

Daniel, P. 'The New Recycling: Economic Theory, IMF Conditionality and Balance of Payments Adjustment in the 1980s' in S. Griffith-Jones and D. Seers, *Monetarism and the Third World*, IDS Bulletin, vol. 13, no. 1 (1981)

Dell, S. and Lawrence, R. *The Balance of Payments Adjustment Process in Developing Countries* (Pergamon, United Nations, New York, 1980)

Dell, S. 'On being Grandmotherly: the Evolution of IMF Conditionality', *Essays in International Finance*, no. 144 (Princeton University, 1981)

Diaz-Alejandro and Bacha, E. 'Financial Markets: a View from the Periphery', paper presented at International Seminar on External Financial Relations, (Santiago de Chile, 19-21 March 1981)

Euromoney, several issues (1978, 1983)

Euromoney, several articles, especially P. Field, D. Shireff and W. Ollard, 'The IMF and the Central Banks Flex their Muscles' and 'Bossing the Markets', *Editorial* (January 1983)

Evans, P. 'Recent Research on Multinational Corporations', *Annual Review of Sociology* (1980) pp. 199-223

Frank, C.R. 'Future Financing of the Capital Needs of Developing Countries', *Towards a New Bretton-Woods Selected Background Papers*, Commonwealth Economic Papers no. 18 (Commonwealth Secretariat, London 1983)

Griffith-Jones, S. 'The Alliance for Progress: an Attempt at Interpretation', *Development and Change*, vol. 10, no. 3 (July 1979)

Griffith-Jones, S. 'The Growth of Multinational Banking, the Euro-currency Market and the Effects on Developing Countries', *Journal of Development Studies*, vol. 16, no. 2 (June 1980)

Griffith-Jones, S. *Compensatory Financing Facility: a Review of its Operation and Proposals for Improvement* (1982) Report to the Group of Twenty Four, UNDP/UNCTAD Studies of International Monetary and Financial Issues for Developing Countries (January 1983)

Helleiner, G.K. (forthcoming) 'South-South Cooperation in the 1980s', *Third World Quarterly* (1983)

*Herrera, J.*E. and Morales, J. 'Opening up to the Outside World and its Effects on the National Economy: the Case of Chile', *IFDA Dossier, 11* (Geneva, Switzerland, September 1979)

Horsefield, J.K. *The International Monetary Fund, 1945-65, Vol I: Chronicle* (IMF, Washington DC, 1969)

Horsefield J.K. (ed.) *The International Monetary Fund, 1945-1965. Vol III: Documents* (IMF, Washington DC, 1969)

ICIDI *Common Crisis: North South: Cooperation for World Recovery* (The Brandt Commission 1983, Pan Books, London and Sydney)

IMF *IMF Survey* (Washington DC, 18 May 1981)

IMF *IMF Survey* (Washington DC, 8 February 1982a)

IMF *International Financial Statistics, Supplement on Fund Accounts*, Supplement Series, no. 3 (1982b)

IMF 'International Capital Markets', Developments and Prospects, 1982, *Occasional Paper 14* (Washington DC, July 1982c)

Inter-American Development Bank, *Economic and Social Progress in Latin America* (Washington DC, 1979)

Johnson, C. 'What are the Prospects for Growth in International Credit Markets?' paper presented to *Financial Times/Banker's World Banking Conference*, 9 December 1982

Kapur, I. 'An analysis of the Supply of Euro-currency Finance to Developing Countries' in *Oxford Bulletin of Economics and Statistics*, vol. 39, no. 3 (1977)

Keynes, J.M. *The General Theory of Employment, Interest and Money* (Macmillan, London, 1936)

Lamfalussy, A. 'Changing Attitudes towards Capital Movements', paper presented at Conference on Changing Perceptions of Economic Policy (Oxford, 27-29 March 1981)

Levinson, J. and Onis, J. *The Alliance that Lost its Way, a Critical Report on the Alliance for Progress* (Archangel Books, Chicago, 1970)

Lipton, M. and Griffith-Jones, S. 'International Lender of Last Resort; are Changes Required?' *Study on the International Financial and Trading System*, background paper, Commonwealth Secretariat (London, 1983)

Mackworth-Young, W. 'Role for International Bond Markets', *Financial Times* (9 May 1983)

McKinnon, R.E. 'The Euro-Currency Market', *Essays in International Finance*, no. 125 (Princeton University, December 1977)

McKinnon, R.E. 'Currency Substitution and Instability in the World Dollar Standard', *American Economic Review* (June 1982)

Morgan Guaranty *World Financial Markets* (several issues)

O'Brien, R. 'Private Bank Lending to Developing Countries', *World Bank Staff Paper*, no. 482 (August 1981)

Parkinson, F. *Latin America, the Cold War and the World Powers, 1945-73* (Sage Publications, 1974)

Polak, J.J. *Thoughts on an International Monetary Fund Based Fully on the SDR*, IMF Pamphlet Series, no. 28 (Washington, 1979)

Prout, C. 'Finance for Developing Countries: an Essay' in S. Strange, *International Monetary Relations*, vol. 2 of *International Economic Relations of the Western World* A. Schonfield (ed.) (Oxford University Press, 1976)

Prebisch, R. 'Commercial Policy in the Underdeveloped Countries', *American Economic Review*, vol. 49, no. 2 (1959)

Prebisch, R. *Towards a New Trade Policy for Development*, report by the Secretary General of UNCTAD, Raul Prebisch, United Nations (New York, 1964)

Prebisch, R. 'La Cooperacion Internacional en el Desarrollo Latinoamericano' in *Problemas Economicos y Sociales de America Latina* (Ediciones Tercer Mundo, Colombia, 1979)

Robinson, J. 'The International Currency Proposals' *Economic Journal* (June September 1943)

Roosa, R.V. 'Economic Instability and Flexible Exchange Rates' in *World Money and National Policies*, Group of 30, occasional paper 12 (New York, 1983)

Rohatyn, F. 'New Bretton-Woods Conference Needed', *Financial Times* (9 May 1983)

Schuler, H.D. 'Evaluation of Risk in International Lending – a Bank Examiner's Perspective', speech of the Federal Reserve Bank of Boston Conference on *Key Issues in International Banking* (October 1977)

Schlesinger, A. 'The Alliance for Progress: a Perspective' in R.G. Hillman and H.J. Rosenbaum (eds.), *Latin America: the Search for a New International Role* (John Wiley and Sons, 1975)

Seers, D. 'Massive Transfers and Mutual Interests', *World Development*, vol. 9, no. 6 (1981)

Seiber, M.J. 'Developing Countries in the Euro-currency Market: a Debt Overhang Escalator' (US Department of Commerce, Washington DC, 1977)

Seiber, M.J. *International Borrowing by Developing Countries*, Pergamon policy studies in economic development (Pergamon Press, 1982)

Solomon. R. 'The Allocation of Oil Deficits', *Brookings Papers on Economic Activity* (Washington DC, Spring 1975)

Solomon, R. *The International Monetary System, 1945-81* (Harper and Row, New York, 1982)

Stewart, F. and Sengupta, A. *Framework for International Financial Cooperation* (Frances Pinter, 1982)

Strange, S. 'IMF; Monetary Managers' in R. Cox and H. Jacobson (eds.), *The Anatomy of Influence* (Yale University Press, 1973)

Sunkel, O. 'External Dependency and National Policy of Development' in *Journal of Development Studies* (October 1969)

Sunkel, O. and Fuenzalida, E. 'Transnationalisation and its National Consequences' in J. Villamil (ed.), *Transnational Capitalism and National Development* (Harvester Press, US Congress, 1979 a Spanish version, published by *Fondo de Cultura Economica*, 1982)

Thorp, R. and Whitehead, L. *Inflation and Stabilisation in Latin America* (Macmillan, 1979)

Triffin, R. *Gold and the Dollar Crisis* (Yale University Press, New Haven, 1960)

Triffin, R. 'Gold and the Dollar Crisis: Yesterday and Tomorrow', *Princeton Essays in International Finance*, no. 132 (1978)

Triffin, R. 'The Future of the International Monetary System' in Proceedings of the Second World Scientific Banking Meeting, *International Financing of Economic Development* (Dubrovnik, 26-31 May 1980)

UNCTAD Secretariat *UNCTAD VI International Financial and Monetary Issues Policy Paper*, TD-278 (Belgrade, June 1983)

US Congress Senate Committee on Foreign Relations, *International Debt, the Banks and US Foreign Policy*, prepared by Karin Lissakers, 95th Congress, 1st Session (Washington DC, 1977)

US Department of Commerce, *Survey of Current Business* (February 1981)

Wallich, H. 'Forces that Drive International Monetary Evolution' in *World Money and National Policies*, Group of 30, occasional paper 12 (New York, 1983)

Wellons, P.A. *Borrowing by Developing Countries on the Euro-currency Market* (OECD Development Centre, Paris, 1977)

Williamson, J. *The Failure of World Monetary Reform* (Thomas Nelson and Sons, 1977)

Williamson, J. 'Keynes and the International Economic Order' paper presented to the Conference on *The Relevance of Keynes's Economics Today* held at King's College, Cambridge, 15-16 July 1983

Williamson, J. 'International Monetary Reform: an Agenda for the 1980s' *Study on the International Financial and Trading System Background Paper* (Commonwealth Secretariat, London, 1983b)

World Bank, *Borrowing in International Capital Markets*, EC-181/172, Second Quarter (Washington DC, 1978)

World Bank, *World Development Report* (1981)

Wright, E.P. 'World Bank Lending for Structural Adjustment', *Finance and Development* (January 1980)

INDEX